Victorious
Healing
and
Growth
Through
God's Grace

Alison R.
Blackwood

TEACH Services, Inc.
PUBLISHING
www.TEACHServices.com • (800) 367-1844

Copyright © 2014 Alison R. Blackwood
Copyright © 2014 TEACH Services, Inc.
ISBN-13: 978-1-4796-0329-9 (Paperback)
ISBN-13: 978-1-4796-0330-5 (ePub)
ISBN-13: 978-1-4796-0331-2 (Mobi)
Library of Congress Control Number: 2014939084

All scripture quotations, unless otherwise indicated, are taken from the King James Version. Public domain.

Published by

TEACH Services, Inc.
P U B L I S H I N G
www.TEACHServices.com • (800) 367-1844

Acknowledgment

Thanks to God for providing us with His precious and priceless gift of salvation and for providing encouraging friendships along the Christian journey.

Table of Contents

Section 3: God's Gift and Humanity's Condition

Section 4: God's Involvement in Our Lives

Section 5: Our Growth

Section 6: Restored and Whole in Christ

Introduction

All around us are the effects of the busy pace of life and the associated complexities found in our relationships. All of this combined can affect our ability to enjoy mental rest. While living in a busy world, our focus can be pulled in different directions, and we can experience mental fatigue. A good night's sleep can be ruined because a person's mind is bombarded by thoughts and memories that carry pain and guilt.

In this book we will review the lives of some Bible characters and see how they dealt with their difficulties. We will explore how some of their attitudes (positive and negative) are still seen today. On this journey we will seek to understand our complex realities in order to find ways to effectively deal with the challenging situations in which we find ourselves. It is hoped that we will discover a variety of ways to direct our efforts and time to finding effective solutions.

Our journey through the pages ahead discusses why it is critical for us to have a correct attitude when dealing

with relational issues and confronting our own weaknesses. We will explore how the solution God has provided for us reassures us of spiritual well-being and equips
us to face the mental exposure in our working relationships. We will look at how our daily interactions and attitudes can affect our ability to accept God's solution. We
will look at why our daily connection to God is critical in
helping us overcome the challenges to which we are daily
exposed and how it encourages the display of the fruit of
the Spirit in our lives. We will walk the very crucial journey of being whole in Jesus, a journey we should never
take for granted.

Section 1:

Life Today

Seeking Balance in a Busy World

*"Thou art my hiding place; thou shalt preserve me
from trouble; thou shalt compass me about with
songs of deliverance." Psalm 32:7*

After an exhausting day accompanied by rush hour as we return home, we often experience fatigue and need to mentally refocus before facing another day.

Some people may feel that they are navigating through traffic as they respond to the demands placed on them by their colleagues, supervisors, and subordinates, who "honk" at those around them to move faster or to move out of the way.

With the many and sometimes conflicting deadlines and demands, unwelcome stress invites itself into our lives. Sometimes it seems that unless we shout, no one hears us or is aware that they might be stepping on our toes in their own quest to survive. But if everyone is shouting and crying for aid, who can hear us and who can help? The answer is found in Isaiah 65:24. God says, "Before they call, I will answer; and while they are yet speaking, I will hear."

But sometimes it is difficult to understand that God is listening. These feelings reveal the need for our belief and trust in our Creator to develop. In Mark 9:24 we read of a man who cried out to God to help his child. He said, "Lord, I believe; help ... mine unbelief." The man acknowledged his weaknesses, but he did not use his limitations as an excuse or a reason not to exercise the faith he already had. We must believe that God will hear us and will help us in our weak areas. If we accept God's hope, our lives will reflect this hope. The extent to which we believe and trust God is important because we live according to what we believe.

Since we represent our beliefs in our actions, we may display a myriad of behaviors in the areas where we doubt and struggle. This can send conflicting signals to those around us and even to ourselves. Because our lives are made up of relationships with other people, it is easy for these relationships to be strained because of contradictory signals. All of this is added to the fast pace of life, where more time is

> *Let us always remember that our individual circumstances are part of a bigger picture, and that God sees the full and complete picture.*

spent on meeting deadlines and less time is spent on thinking about the impact of our actions on others.

As we go about our daily routine, let us be aware of how we treat the people with whom we interact. Sometimes there is such a big priority on achieving and moving ahead in life that our relationships with others can be negatively affected. Amidst our challenges and day-to-day routines, God wants us to come to Him and experience the comfort He alone provides. Though this may be difficult to do at times, we must aim to be like the man who asked God to help his unbelief. We need to ask God to help us in our areas of doubt. Let us always remember that our individual circumstances are part of a bigger picture, and that God sees the full and complete picture.

God knows and understands our struggles and pains, and He will offer us the refuge we need as we live each day. All we need to do is simply believe and trust that He is there for us.

Facing the Challenges of Life

"The angel of the LORD *encampeth round about
them that fear him, and delivereth them."*
Psalm 34:7

While holding her baby and walking next to her three-year-old daughter, a mother was confronted by a dog, which proceeded to jump all around her and her children. Clinging to her mother, the three-year-old girl was trying in her own way to get out of the reach of the dog, but the dog was bigger than the child.

The shouts from the woman did not distract the dog, but people living in the houses nearby heard the cries and came to their rescue. It is interesting to note that the woman and her two children were helpless until other people got involved in their situation and drove the dog away.

Unlike the man who came to Jesus knowing his problem (Mark 9:24), the woman was not aware that there was danger until the dog confronted her. She had no time to prepare or mentally brace herself for the danger. Sometimes experiences in life can leave us disoriented for a while. Sometimes it seems that we find ourselves trying to go in different directions at the same time. We try to spin at the pace created by a busy life, and it can sometimes cause us to faint or even to forget in which direction we should go.

Like the woman and her children, we can also be caught off guard by the dangers that confront us each day. We should not wait to go to Jesus when we feel a specific need, for we need God to walk with us at all times throughout the day. We need to ask Jesus to give us His wisdom and knowledge to deal with difficult situations, but we should not wait until the last moment to ask for guidance.

We are not equipped to face the problems alone when they arise. We need God's protection, even if things appear to be calm. We may not feel threatened by an angry dog, but we will face many unexpected challenges. If we strive to keep God's Word in our hearts, the Holy Spirit can bring to our remembrance Bible verses like "The LORD shall fight for you, and ye shall hold your peace" (Exod. 14:14), which will remind us not to depend on our own wisdom in these circumstances.

We need to be prudent in our daily associations. First Peter 5:8 tells us to "be sober, be vigilant." Living in this world with the threat of our "adversary the devil, as a roaring lion ... seeking whom he may devour" (1 Peter 5:8), it should be realized that we need to seek God's guidance for everything, even when decisions seem insignificant.

Though there are some situations we can't avoid, we can take comfort in the fact that help is always available to us. God "encamps" around those who fear Him, and He will deliver us from all our challenges if we daily walk with Him.

Difficulties That Could Arise in Our Relationships

"Come unto me, all ye that labour and are heavy laden, and I will give you rest." Matthew 11:28

Our knowledge and understanding of situations can impact the ways in which we deal with circumstances. Imagine seeing a cherished vase fall from the hands of someone we know. If we were aware that the person, while trying to save the vase from falling, lost their balance and their hand jolted resulting in the vase falling to the ground, we would possibly be sympathetic towards the person. We may, however, have opposite feelings if we felt the person willingly broke the vase or if the person tried to excuse what they did or downplay our hurt.

If we have traveled a road several times, it is realistic for us to expect to find the road accessible. But imagine while traveling the familiar road, we reach an impassable part of the road, and there were no warning signs. Similarly, this unexpected blockage can occur in relationships.

We expect our friends to be trustworthy, our family members to be dependable, and our colleagues to be team-oriented. These expectations are justifiable, but when we are hurt, we may struggle with the trust we placed in these people. When the relationship reaches a roadblock with or without warning, the dependable may become undependable.

If we realize that the "blockage" is not deliberate and that our friend needs our patience during a difficult time in his or her life, we are likely to be more sympathetic.

But if we realize that the person willfully did something to hurt us (such as breaking the vase), it can cause sadness and deep disappointment.

Having relationships with each other is a fundamental part of our human existence. And during such fundamental interactions, we can, at times, experience pain and hurt. It is always easy when things are going well in our relationships, but it is the conflicts that we may wish to avoid. However, these same conflicts can provide an opportunity for growth, as parties genuinely seek to address any existing misunderstandings.

If we have invested much effort in the relationship, the process to recovery may seem more difficult. We may question the things we once believed, and we may wrestle with accepting the unwelcome changes.

> *Reading the Bible gives us a correct understanding of the sin problem and helps us to focus on seeking God's solutions.*

We all need rest, and we all need assurance. When we face disappointments in relationships, we may feel mentally burdened. But there is hope. Jesus provides comfort for the hurting.

When we look at things on the surface, it is easy to get angry and frustrated, but reading the Bible gives us a correct understanding of the sin problem and helps us to focus on seeking God's solutions. We shift our focus from anger—which can deplete our strength and ability to cope—to seeking the path of restoration. Thankfully, the Holy Spirit is with us to ease this transition.

The delicate balance of still being able to nurture healthy relationships yet adjust expectations and not be overcome by human weaknesses is a process of growth. After being hurt, it is worth the effort to learn to smile again.

God provides avenues for us to heal and move on and connect with others, be it through trained Christian counselors, with family, with friends, or through church and community activities. These interactions can help us to continue along the path of life. Our restoration will involve determining if we can rebuild the damaged road (relationship), or if we need to readjust our focus and reverse from the impassable road and change direction.

We do not have to do something wrong to feel emotional pain, but emotional pain is a reminder of the ills of sin. With God's help, we can decide not to hurt people the way we may have been hurt.

We also should be sensitive to the needs of others, since unknowingly we too may have hurt others causing us to need to receive forgiveness from a cherished friend. Though we may have experienced disappointments, let us seek to rise above our own hurts and be positive influences to others. With the help of God, let us always endeavor to contribute to the healing in ourselves and in others.

Section 2:

Learning From Biblical Experiences

Inspiration in Difficulty

"All scripture is given by inspiration of God, and is profitable for doctrine, for reproof, for correction, for instruction in righteousness." 2 Timothy 3:16

In the work environment, interactions occur between persons with varying backgrounds, and persons are sometimes expected—at short notice—to adjust to new work mates and team members yet maintain focus and continue to meet the stipulated output in a short timeframe.

When we study the Bible, we see how Bible characters dealt with being in authority, being subject to the authority of others, or working alongside others. This insight can offer us understanding and guidance in how we can deal with team members in our work environment.

In the Bible we also read of people who had developed meaningful relationships. Though Jonathan's father hated David, Jonathan recognized the genuine and kind person David was. Their friendship became very strong, and they promised to be kind to each other's family (1 Sam. 18:3, 4; 19:4; 20:42). Ruth valued the friendship of her mother-in-law, so she willingly left her native home and followed Naomi back to her homeland (Ruth 1:16, 17).

The Shunammite woman observed that Elisha travelled far distances and realized that having a room in which to rest would help him, so she and her husband prepared a room for Elisha to rest in on his journeys (2 Kings 4:8–11). Paul appreciated the friendship of Timothy, and he embraced Timothy as his spiritual son (1 Tim. 1:2, 18).

Amidst the challenges, the workplace also provides opportunities for us to develop healthy, meaningful, and lifelong relationships. We can find many avenues for us to grow in different aspects of our lives.

Interacting with others in difficult situations is only one of the many challenges we may face on a day-to-day basis. So having decided to live the Christian life, we all need encouragement in order to hold on and not let "the cares of this world" (Mark 4:19) get us down. Understanding how people recorded in the Bible dealt with their challenges can help us as we face our challenges today. Both James 5:17, which refers to Elias (Elijah), and Acts 14:15, which refers to Barnabas and Paul, tell us that these biblical persons had "passions" like us. These men dealt with the same feelings and difficulties that we Christians struggle with today. Because the Bible tells us that they eventually triumphed over their passions, it gives us hope that we can succeed as well.

> *A trail, stamped out in the grass from many feet that walked that way before, provides strength and confidence for those coming after.*

A trail, stamped out in the grass from many feet that walked that way before, provides strength and confidence for those coming after. The trail makes it easier to follow. As we read about others in the Bible who grew in faith, our faith in God will also grow.

People recorded in the Bible experienced the conflict between good and evil; each one faced the struggle to choose to go their own way or God's way. They confronted and overcame obstacles when standing up for the right. They were also exposed to mental attacks through accusations, which resulted in disappointments, uncertainty, discouragement, and emotional pain.

They did not allow the wrong to change their direction; they endured great challenges and emerged standing firm in their faith in God. They experienced God's healing and restorative power as they went through their daily activities. We hear in the pages of the Bible that we too can make it. It is possible to be like them; it is possible to pull through our difficulties and stay true to our beliefs. Their stories inspire us to keep on believing even in times of stress, conflict, uncertainty, and the unknown.

These stories also remind us that God, who took care of them, is taking care of us as well. This can help us gain the confidence to live with the zeal and determination that salvation has made possible for everyone. We are assured that God can restore us and save us.

The Importance of Faith

"For by [faith] the elders obtained a good report."
Hebrews 11:2

Walking into the principal's office of the high school I had attended many years ago, I gazed at the pictures of the past students who had won scholarships and obtained a good report because of their academic successes. Some of the faces I knew, and I recounted the sacrifices they had made in order to achieve. But there is a greater achievement God desires all of us to experience. It is, therefore, an entirely different and more beautiful thing when our Creator acknowledges our good work. We are taught in school what we need to do to reach success, but what exactly do we need to do to obtain God's approval?

The answer is found in Hebrews 10:38 where we are told, "the just shall live by faith," and in Hebrews 12:2 which says that we should look "unto Jesus the author and finisher of our faith." Jesus provides the faith we are seeking. In faith we ask for God's forgiveness of our sins, in faith we accept God's forgiveness, and through faith we walk as people who are forgiven.

My travel experiences have reinforced to me the importance of faith. After checking in at an airport to return home from a meeting, my colleague and I hadn't bargained for the ensuing delay. Because of the unexpected delay and since the airport staff was unable to tell us the exact departure time of the flight, we went through immigration and customs, headed for the departure lounge, and waited there. We listened attentively to the announcements relating to departing flights and all our activities were conducted within hearing distance of the loud speakers. It didn't matter what we were doing, we were always ready to cease these activities once the flight was announced. After all, we had to depend on that airline to get home. In the same way we were dependent on the announcements to tell us what was happening, we depend on and look to Jesus to guide us along the road of life.

> *There are no sweeter words to hear than the words of affirmation "Well done" from our Lord.*

At school, students are successful when they are committed to the tasks and are receptive to the instructions given by teachers, who patiently work with and guide the students. At the end of the school year, children anxiously wait to receive their report cards. Some children present their report cards to their parents with joy, while others look for the right time to break the news of a not-so-favorable report.

Like the students who receive good reports from their teachers, the Bible states that the elders obtained a good report. This report was based on the work God was doing in their lives and how well they yielded themselves in obedience to Him.

Imagine receiving positive feedback from the Creator, who made us, who knows the real us, who knows every sin we have ever committed (Ps. 69:5), who can read our thoughts (Ps. 139:2), and who can see us in our entirety. A good report from the One who knows us and accepts us is more important than any other affirmation. The positive report the elders received was obtained because of their faith in Him. There are no sweeter words to hear than the words of affirmation "Well done" (Matt. 25:21) from our Lord. Let us each actively strive to exercise our faith in Him so that we too can be rewarded as the elders recorded in Hebrews were rewarded.

God's Creative Power

"Through faith we understand that the worlds
were framed by the word of God, so that things
which are seen were not made of things which do
appear." Hebrews 11:3

One night a little boy dropped his mother's flashlight, and it stopped working. The mother knew that in order to get it fixed she needed to send it to someone who understood its functions and mechanics. It couldn't be fixed by chance or by a series of random events.

In a similar way, how do we know God created the worlds? We weren't there when God performed His creative work. But we have enough evidence to see that the world was formed by a Master Creator. It is easy to see that we have a Creator who is able to design the most intricate, immensely complex, fascinating, and mind-boggling things.

These things are so wonderful that people spend their lives specializing in trying to understand various aspects of creation, but they have yet to discover more about God's creation! The discoveries only identify other mysteries that initiate increasing research topics for other curious and brilliant minds to attempt to unravel.

With this evidence in mind, our faith leads us to believe that "in the beginning God created the heaven and the earth" (Gen. 1:1), and this faith allows us to acknowledge God as our Creator. Throughout the Bible we read other beautiful verses that record God's creative power. For example, Psalm 19:1 tells us, "The heavens declare the glory of God; and the firmament sheweth his handywork."

Psalm 24:1 tells us, "The earth is the Lord's, and the fulness thereof; the world, and they that dwell therein."

This text acknowledges God's ownership of us. God reveals to us that He is God, that there is no other like Him, and that He made everything and is above everything.

This fundamental understanding is important because as we grasp the story of how sin entered the perfect world, we can see God as our Redeemer, who is eternal (Rev. 1:8) and is working for us and through us to restore us to what He intended us to be. As part of "the whole armour of God" (Eph. 6:11), faith as a shield is needed to "quench all the fiery darts of the wicked" (Eph. 6:16); these darts of doubt often lead to speculation about the creative authority of God.

Like the flashlight broken after falling to the ground, our world also became dark because of sin, and it required Someone who knew how to fix the problem to illuminate our minds. That Someone is Jesus, who engraved us "upon the palms of [His] hands" (Isa. 49:16) when He died for us. It is wonderful to know God made the world for us to live in, and that we are also "fearfully and wonderfully made" by Him (Ps. 139:14).

Obedience to God

"By faith Abel offered unto God a more excellent
sacrifice than Cain, by which he obtained witness
that he was righteous, God testifying of his gifts:
and by it he being dead yet speaketh."
Hebrews 11:4

On my last day of work at a previous employer, my colleague called me from my desk and led me to the open area in the office. Several smiling faces met me there. After bidding me farewell, my boss handed me a gift bag containing a beautiful portfolio, which was exactly what I wanted.

I had planned to purchase one for myself. I don't recall telling anyone I wanted a portfolio, but my friends made the effort to find out what would please me, and that made such a difference to me.

But even more important, God is happy when we seek to please Him. Obeying God and doing what is pleasing to Him is an integral part of the Christian's life. Abel obeyed God because he believed in God and was compelled by his belief to follow God's instructions. His faith was converted into action and produced a testimony of obedience, "And the LORD had respect unto Abel and to his offering" (Gen. 4:4).

Cain was angry because Abel's sacrifice was accepted, and because of this jealousy, Cain killed Abel (Gen. 4:8).

Cain reacted out of emotion and stubbornness and gave God the gift he felt comfortable giving. For Cain, the decision did not consider God's requirements; it was all about what Cain wanted to do.

The same self-gratifying spirit that caused Cain to give God what he pleased was the same spirit that caused

Cain to strike his brother. Abel was a reminder of what Cain should be, a reminder that Cain impulsively sought to silence. But God took note of Abel's gift of faith, and God takes note of ours today as well.

God gives us the strength to offer to Him the gift He desires of us, even if it is more than we are initially comfortable giving. Then as our growth in Christ continues, the things that caused us pain to give up will soon bring us joy as we come to fully understand how much it pleases the God we love.

Receiving God's Commendation

*"By faith Enoch was translated that he should not
see death; and was not found, because God had
translated him: for before his translation he had
this testimony, that he pleased God."*
Hebrews 11:5

Before boarding the airplane, I waited in line to go through the security checkpoint. As I approached the X-ray machine, I removed my shoes and placed them, along with my carry-on luggage, on the conveyor belt. After walking through the metal detector, a pleasant customs officer greeted me with a smile and said, "You made it." These are very encouraging words to a traveler. This experience caused me to reflect on the wonderful heavenly meeting that would have occurred between God and Enoch.

Enoch lived in the atmosphere of God's presence while on earth, and God gave Enoch the privilege to continue their relationship without seeing death. Genesis 5:24 says, "Enoch walked with God," so Enoch had learned that God "hath shewed thee, O man, what is good; and what doth the LORD require of thee, but to do justly, and to love mercy, and to walk humbly with thy God?" (Micah 6:8).

Amos 3:3 says, "Can two walk together, except they be agreed?" This means that since Enoch walked with God, he had already wholeheartedly accepted God's leading and submitted to His will. Meanwhile, Exodus 33:20 tells us that no one can see God's face and live. So while Enoch was on earth, faith provided the bridge for Enoch to see God. And today our walk on earth is also "by faith, not by sight" (2 Cor. 5:7).

We cannot fully comprehend who God is, but like Enoch we will one day see God and live. God saw and knew the core of Enoch and granted Enoch the privilege of continued communion with Him.

This communion can start any day, any moment. God is always interested in creating a similar relationship with us as He had with Enoch. In Philippians 3:10 Paul shares his desire to "know [Christ], and the power of his resurrection." This is what every Christian desires—to live eternally with God. Paul also said he desired to know "the fellowship of his sufferings," which indicated that Paul was willing to accept whatever Jesus allowed to come into his life.

Enoch was not comparing himself to people but to the standard set by God.

There is a transforming process occurring in us along the Christian path, as we willingly allow ourselves to be fully exposed to God and accept the way in which God sees us.

I can imagine seeing Enoch on earth with a strong desire to be in God's presence, to learn more about God, and to please God in all his conversations, actions, and thoughts. Enoch was not focused on how close to sin he could live and yet be saved; he was focused on how close to God he could live irrespective of the sinful influences. Enoch was not comparing himself to people but to the standard set by God.

It is a blessing to have such an example as Enoch and to know that God honors our faith and desire to know Him.

Believing What God Says

"But without faith it is impossible to please him:
for he that cometh to God must believe that he is,
and that he is a rewarder of them that diligently
seek him." Hebrews 11:6

"Go and wash in Jordan seven times, and thy flesh shall come again to thee, and thou shalt be clean" (2 Kings 5:10). The prophet's message was clear. Naaman, the courageous captain of an army, was upset. He had expected to be met personally by the prophet, and he did not like being greeted by a servant with the message. But that wasn't all that was making him angry. He was also angry because he was instructed to wash in the river Jordan when he had nicer rivers at home (see 2 Kings 5:11, 12).

Naaman desired and hoped to be healed. Fortunately, after following the advice of a trusted servant, Naaman reconsidered his decision and dipped in the river Jordan seven times as directed (see 2 Kings 5:13, 14), and he experienced the healing he was seeking.

Naaman's decision to travel so far showed he did have some belief in God's ability to heal, but his faith had to go further to believe God enough to do it God's way. He needed to submit to God and obey God completely. After all, it wasn't just any river; it was the river God instructed him to go into. It was not any amount of times he felt like dipping; it was seven times as God directed.

Shortcuts would not have provided Naaman with the desired results, and he needed to develop his faith before seeing the results of the miracle of healing. This faith propelled him to get up and move forward, and with the influence and advice of his servant, Naaman's faith grew stronger. As we can see from his healing, God was pleased with Naaman's faith.

This story assures us that God has a gift for those serious about finding Him. God is happy when we trust Him. Having faith and studying God's Word are connected. Trying to travel the Christian journey without reading God's Word and without being led by the Holy Spirit is like trying to drive a car into unknown territory without a road map and without fuel. Psalm 119:105 says that God's "word is a lamp unto my feet, and a light unto my path," and Proverbs 4:18 says, "the path of the just is as the shining light, that shineth more and more unto the perfect day." As we study and seek God, He reveals Himself to us, and our understanding of who He is and of His will for our lives becomes clearer each day.

For the busy Christians today, the question may arise, how can I walk in faith at home, on the road in busy traffic, on the job, and when I am confronted with conflicts? How can faith be manifested in every aspect of my life? With the determination like Daniel, who focused on God's requirement and "purposed in his heart" to obey God (Dan. 1:8), we travel the Christian journey by making one decision at a time, each decision being guided by biblical teachings. And with each decision we pray for God to guide us and to enlighten our intellectual capacities.

God helps us to live with the understanding that our survival is wrapped up in Him, that the time we spend with Him to build our relationship is more important than any other thing we can do, and that He will make Himself known to us as we search for Him daily and seek after righteousness and truth. There are treasures awaiting us when we truly believe and trust in God's Word.

Listening to God

"By faith Noah, being warned of God of things not seen as yet, moved with fear, prepared an ark to the saving of his house; by the which he condemned the world, and became heir of the righteousness which is by faith." Hebrews 11:7

At the supermarket there were long lines of people with carts filled with items such as canned food, candles, flashlights, and batteries. They were waiting to pay for their supplies in preparation for the hurricane expected to "hit" within the next twenty-four hours. Having experienced the devastation of storms and hurricanes before, people took the warnings seriously and made preparations. Humankind takes these warnings seriously now, but that was not always the case.

Genesis 6:5 tells us "that the wickedness of man was great in the earth, and that every imagination of the thoughts of his heart was only evil continually." In this environment God found Noah, "a just man and perfect in his generations ... [who] walked with God" (Gen. 6:9) and "found grace in the eyes of the LORD" (Gen. 6:8).

In 1 Peter 3:20 we see that while the ark was being built, God exercised patience with those who did not believe. Second Peter 2:5 describes Noah as "a preacher of righteousness," which shows that God desires for others to be saved, and through Noah, God proclaimed His Word to the people of the day.

Today, those who have never experienced the devastation of a hurricane may be tempted to take a hurricane warning lightly. Genesis 2:5, 6 reveal that the people alive then had never seen rain, but the plants were watered by "a mist from the earth."

Noah, having never seen rain, built the ark based on God's Word, long before the first sign of a rain cloud. God's Word was more important to Noah than what he had seen, and his life of obedience was a testimony to those around him that something unusual was about to happen.

Noah acted from his conviction, and being laughed at and taunted for living opposite to those around him didn't stop Noah from doing what God had convicted him to do; Noah remained focused. The saving of Noah and his household required obedience in action right through to getting onto the ark.

Interestingly, Matthew 7:15, 16 and 1 John 4:1 warn us about false prophets; as God's children we have to be in tune with God, just like Noah, to know God's voice. God had provided Noah with the spirit of discernment that allowed him to see beyond deception and rightfully identify God's voice. The time Noah spent praying to God ultimately

> *People desiring God's presence have sought Him and have set their eyes on Him as they move in His direction.*

resulted in a two-way communication, and when God spoke to Noah, Noah obeyed.

Our obedience to God will be something we desire to do and look forward to doing. We can also look to the example of the psalmist: "I delight to do thy will, O my God: yea, thy law is within my heart" (Ps. 40:8). Noah is a shining example of content obedience, despite what the world around us says or does.

Plants that are growing in a dark place will grow in the direction from which light is emitted; similarly, in this world darkened by sin, people desiring God's presence have sought Him and have set their eyes on Him as they move in His direction.

Abraham's Example

"By faith Abraham, when he was called to go out into a place which he should after receive for an inheritance, obeyed; and he went out, not knowing whither he went." Hebrews 11:8

Abraham was born ten generations after Noah (see Gen. 9:18; Gen. 11:10–26). Genesis does not give many details about the lives of those who lived between Noah and Abraham's generations, but from Genesis 11:3–6 we see that the people were looking to build a tower to "reach unto heaven." People were focused on living their own way, and God looked for someone to carry His message, so God found Abraham.

Leaving friends and family for extended periods of time can be emotionally unsettling. Uprooting, packing, and moving to another place with which we may have some degree of familiarity is stressful enough, but packing up and moving to a place to which we have never been and which we don't know requires a lot of faith.

Today, travel is a normal part of many people's lives. With maps, the Internet, travel agents, and travel guides, we can generally get a good picture about the places we intend to visit ahead of our trip.

In Abraham's time there wasn't such an array of information available to a traveler. Abraham started out on his journey without knowledge of his final destination. He knew that the place he was going was a place God wanted him to be, and he had to tell his family and friends goodbye with no guarantee he would ever see them again. Abraham's faith was strengthened as he obeyed God's voice, and Abraham left the details in God's hand.

God worked through the earthly leading to help Abraham understand who He is. The process of developing and leaning on God continued as Abraham traveled to the land of promise, and it even continued while in the land of promise. Abraham maintained his willingness to listen and obey God's commands. In Genesis 18:1, 6 we read that Abraham and Sarah dwelt in tents. Tents suggest a temporary state of existence, as they were easy to take down should God instruct Abraham to go somewhere new.

Hebrews 11:10 tells us that Abraham "looked for a city which hath foundations, whose builder and maker is God." So although Abraham lived in the land to which God said he should go and enjoyed all its physical blessings, he kept his mind on and looked towards the heavenly Canaan, built by God.

With the many natural disasters that have affected this earth, we do realize that the world is a very unstable place in which to live. With the increase in hurricanes, earthquakes, tidal waves, and volcanic eruptions, many people have now seen the sudden destruction of properties that took them years to build.

Abraham wished to find a city with a permanent foundation, where "neither moth nor rust doth corrupt, and where thieves do not break through nor steal" (Matt. 6:20). He looked forward to living in the "new Jerusalem" (Rev. 21:2), where he would be with Jesus.

We should be inspired to be like Abraham, for Abraham constantly strived to connect with God and keep focused on his real and final destination.

Sarah and Abraham's Faith

"Through faith also Sara herself received strength
to conceive seed, and was delivered of a child
when she was past age, because she judged him
faithful who had promised." Hebrews 11:11

In Genesis 16:3 we read that Sarah tried to "help out" God by giving her handmaiden to Abraham to be his wife in order to fulfill the promise. Sarah's point of unbelief saw her developing an alternative plan in order to obtain the promise. So although she believed what God said, Sarah still depended on her own abilities and made the decision to give God assistance.

Paul explained in Hebrews 11:11 that faith provided Sarah with strength to conceive Isaac. It is plain to see then that this verse gives us hope! It is so encouraging to know that though she and Abraham made mistakes in the past, Sarah and Abraham are recorded as persons with faith.

Anyone who has had to wait a long time for a desired outcome can start to understand some of the emotions with which Sarah must have struggled. As our belief in God is strengthened, we will accept that God also has the "how" sorted out, and in our moments of trying to determine what God expects of us, we will submit to God to ensure our actions are not contrary to His bigger plan and bigger requirements.

We need God's help to know when belief requires action, like Abraham traveling to the land of promise,

> *We need God's help to know when belief requires action, like Abraham traveling to the land of promise, and when belief requires waiting.*

and when belief requires waiting. We need God's strength to help us to act accordingly. When Sarah conceived, she couldn't take any credit for the conception and birth of Isaac. It was God's working to fulfill the promise He had made. It took a long time for Abraham and Sarah to see the fruit, and during the time of disappointment and waiting, Sarah's faith and acceptance of God's leading must have developed.

In Hebrews 11:12 we are told, "Therefore sprang there even of one, and him as good as dead, so many as the stars of the sky in multitude, and as the sand which is by the sea shore innumerable." From one child a great nation was born, and God's promise to Abraham was fulfilled. It wasn't easy for Abraham to live with the knowledge of a promise but the reality of no child. To go from holding onto a hope to seeing the plans unfold before his eyes must have caused him to feel a stronger bond to God. It would have reinforced and strengthened Abraham's resolve of God's goodness. Abraham had grown to depend fully on God, and we see the realization of God's promise in Hebrews 11:12.

The Bible does not paint a picture of ease or of perfect human beings, but we see men and women who were determined to hold onto God's promises and make it through the uncertainties and doubts. We can see that God truly honored and rewarded Sarah and Abraham's faith.

We need to understand that our "help cometh from the LORD" (Ps. 121:2). It is important to acknowledge that God has and will continue to fulfill His promises to us, as He did for Abraham and Sarah.

The Need for Healing

"Finally, be ye all of one mind, having compassion one of another, love as brethren, be pitiful, be courteous: Not rendering evil for evil, or railing for railing: but contrariwise blessing; knowing that ye are thereunto called, that ye should inherit a blessing." 1 Peter 3:8, 9

It is not a coincidence that at times we feel mentally tired and emotionally drained. Spiritual battles are also manifested through criticism, accusations, and blame. The book of Genesis introduces us to a conflict that occurred in the Garden of Eden. Genesis 3:4 informs us that the serpent planted seeds of doubt in Eve's mind about God; the serpent misrepresented the truth with the aim to deceive, and he misrepresented the consequences of disobedience.

When sin entered the world, decay, disappointment, and pain started to compete with the perfect beauty, tranquility, and peace previously experienced by Adam and Eve. Instead of harmony between brothers, conflict and jealousy manifested itself in the relationship between Cain and Abel, which ended in

> *Without God's intervention life would have become a meaningless and hopeless existence.*

murder (Gen. 4:8). With the death of their son, Adam and Eve experienced pain and loss; emotions that then became a part of the human experience.

It must have been difficult for Adam and Eve to leave such beauty and perfection in the Garden of Eden and enter a world of chaos, evil, and death. Although Adam and

Eve had to leave the garden because of their disobedience, Jesus was planning and organizing to pay the sin debt. Genesis 3:15 provides encouragement and the assurance that though people will experience bruises, there will be healing and triumph. Hebrews 5:9 states that Jesus "became the author of eternal salvation unto all them that obey him." Without God's intervention life would have become a meaningless and hopeless existence.

Jesus is fulfilling His promise and has put the plan of salvation into action. We live in a world where people do not always deliver on their promises, but Adam and Eve died with the assurance that God wouldn't forget the promise He made. Psalm 89:34 says, "My covenant will I not break, nor alter the thing that is gone out of my lips." God did not leave the world to spin out of control. There are many biblical examples of how God worked with His children to counter the effects of the bad and support the growth and development of the good. It is in His ability to heal our damaged spirits that we can find the strength to carry on and maintain healthy relationships.

But it can be difficult to maintain or even think about maintaining healthy relationships in some work environments. Nurturing our communication skills and having "compassion one of another," as Peter instructs us to do, can be difficult to do when alongside the pressures of the workplace. However, long before entering the work world, we learn by associations in our families how to deal with each other. Strong and loving family relationships help us deal with difficult working relationships and can teach us loving communication skills.

After spending so much time in a work environment, it is clear that our home and work life do influence each other. Irrespective of the origin of the negative stimuli, we need to explore ways to make sure the negative influences are not translated or spread to other areas of our lives.

Though everyone may not have had the benefit of a nurturing family, God our Father lovingly draws us all to Himself. God teaches His children how to nurture others, and God also brings persons into His children's lives to show His children good examples. God can fill the voids in each of our lives. We can learn lessons from Abraham's life. God was able to say of Abraham, "For I know him, that he will command his children and his household after him, and they shall keep the way of the LORD, to do justice and judgment; that the LORD may bring upon Abraham that which he hath spoken of him" (Gen. 18:19).

Today we can be assured that God has pronounced a blessing on our lives through His plan of salvation; we just need to accept His plan. This blessing promotes hope among us and helps in our healing and restoration. This blessing also helps us become a conduit of God's love, healing, and restoration to others.

Section 3:

God's Gift and Humanity's Condition

Paid in Full

*"For the wages of sin is death; but the gift of God
is eternal life through Jesus Christ our Lord."*
Romans 6:23

Imagine someone's mortgage payments are due, but he or she has no money and is faced with having to leave his or her home permanently. Imagine the person cries out for help and then someone comes along and promises to pay his or her mortgage in full. When sin entered the world, things had to be made right. Romans 3:23 says, "all have sinned, and come short of the glory of God." Death is the payment for sin, and humankind urgently requires a remedy that must be found outside of ourselves. The cost is too great for our shoulders to bear.

Thankfully, God provided this remedy to us as a gift through His grace. When Jesus died He took care of the need for justice to be done. Jesus delivered us from the bondage of sin and provided a way out for a lost world. Jesus bore the consequences of our sin, and He bore our sentence of death. We owe Jesus everything.

After we are convicted of our need for Christ and accept His salvation, our efforts to make ourselves right are replaced with hope in Christ, and we are no longer consumed by hopelessness. We depend on Jesus' righteousness to save us instead of our own righteousness. Depending on our own righteousness or trying to hide and cover our guilt will cause us to lose our way.

God's gift of salvation can't be repaid. We are to accept God's gift in gratitude and nurture a desire and willingness to share God's healing love with others. God gives us peace, not because we are sinless, but because His grace allows us to be free of guilt. Jesus has taken the bitter payment for our sins, and we can walk free of its terrible weight.

If we try to justify ourselves and make things right by how we live, what we have, what we can do, or what we achieve, we will always find ourselves discontented and searching for something more. Any attempts we make outside of Jesus will not have any eternal value. Romans 8:1 says, "There is therefore now no condemnation to them which are in Christ Jesus." Freedom from sin cannot be found outside of Jesus Christ.

So with the void filled, in God's strength we can daily overcome our human weaknesses and challenges and obey God's Word. But it is during our struggles that the enemy may try to make us lose sight of

> *God's sacrifice provides the avenue for forgiveness, restoration, and healing to occur in our relationships.*

Christ's righteousness and tempt us to fight on our own. And the enemy may try to discourage us by reminding us of past sins and failures.

As we see things through God's eyes, we rise above the guilt. We hold onto hope amidst our struggles, and Christ reassures us of His love and guidance. We are not alone in this fight. God provides support to help us make it through. God wants us to pray to Him, read the Bible, and follow the leading of the Holy Spirit. Like Paul, we say, "For I am not ashamed of the gospel of Christ: for it is the power of God unto salvation to every one that believeth" (Rom. 1:16).

God's sacrifice provides the avenue for forgiveness,

restoration, and healing to occur in our relationships. It is a joy to know that we are forgiven and no longer have to carry the weight of imperfections and guilt.

When Jesus tells us we are forgiven, we can enter into His joy and peace. God has given us clearance, and we can rest in His acceptance. Like an overdue mortgage, our sins are paid in full by the blood of Christ.

From Guilt to Forgiveness

*"Being justified freely by his grace through the
redemption that is in Christ Jesus." Romans 3:24*

In Zechariah 3:3 we see a picture of a man dressed
in filthy garments. He was being accused (Zech. 3:1). If
no hope could be found for the high priest, he would be
convicted of sin and condemned. The accuser identified
the high priest's faults to expose his unworthiness, to
give reasons for the high priest's destruction, and to
show why the high priest should not receive healing
and restoration. But although the high priest was accused and his condition was worthy of death, the LORD
stood up for the high priest (Zech. 3:2). The high priest
did not stay in his pitiful condition. God cleaned him
up (Zech. 3:4).

We are advised in Hebrews 4:16 to "come boldly unto
the throne of grace, that we may obtain mercy, and find
grace to help in time of need." Having been offered the gift
of life, people over the centuries have had the choice to
either accept or reject the gift. However, it can sometimes
be difficult to accept this gift because we cannot let go of
the guilt we are experiencing and enjoy the forgiveness
God is willing to give to all of us.

In John 18:10 we read about Simon Peter, who was
quick to defend Jesus and cut off the ear of the servant.
Peter was very self-confident, and he was willing to physi-
cally fight for Jesus, but Peter didn't understand the fight
that Jesus wanted Peter to win was the fight against self.
After all, Peter was sure that he would never deny Jesus,
but since Peter had yet to figure out a solution other than
the physical fight, Peter was depending on fulfilling his

word in his own strength. Yet, under mental and spiritual pressure, Peter buckled and denied Jesus (John 18:27). Due to this experience, Peter experienced pain and guilt, and he "wept bitterly" (Matt. 26:75).

In Luke 22:47, 48 we read that Judas betrayed Jesus. Unlike Peter, who denied Jesus spontaneously because of overconfidence with no plan to sin, Judas plotted his betrayal of Jesus. Judas' sin was premeditated, and he sought personal gain. In Matthew 26:14–16 we read, "Then one of the twelve, called Judas Iscariot, went unto the chief priests, And said unto them, What will ye give me, and I will deliver him unto you? And they covenanted with him for thirty pieces of silver. And from that time he sought opportunity to betray him."

In Matthew 26:47–50 we read that Judas led the soldiers to Jesus and identified Jesus with a kiss. Judas had an agenda; Peter had none. But Judas did not plan for the ensuing guilt. Sadly, Judas continued on the downward spiral. Like Peter, who felt guilty after denying Jesus, Judas was also tormented from the guilt of betraying Jesus. Both Judas and Peter knew and acknowledged they had failed, but they reacted to this knowledge differently, and their reactions made the difference in the outcome of their lives.

In Matthew 27:3 we see Judas humanly trying to make things right by returning the payment he had received for betraying Jesus. Judas was consumed by the emotional torment and pain that came from his guilt, and because he was unable to live with the guilt from his sinful actions, he hanged himself (Matt. 27:5). If not dealt with, guilt can torment our minds.

Peter, however, acknowledged his wrong and continued on to ask and receive forgiveness, and it was a turning point in his life. In areas Peter thought he was strong, the circumstance revealed his weaknesses. After that situation he learned to depend on God's strength instead of his own. Judas died consumed by his guilt, but Peter was freed from its weight.

A look at the two criminals who hung on the crosses beside Jesus also shows two responses to Jesus' offer of salvation. One criminal felt no conviction of his sin and dared Jesus to save them (see Luke 23:39). The other criminal acknowledged his sin and, like Peter, held onto the salvation Jesus offered (see Luke 23:40–43).

The enemy wants us to either be overwhelmed by sin like Judas or be indifferent to sin like the criminal on the cross. The enemy wants us to believe that we should only go the downward spiral and be destroyed as a result of our sins. In both states people do not seek from Jesus forgiveness of sins. By using accusations and discouragement, the enemy is trying to convince us to accept death. Yes, it is death that we really deserve, but it is a penalty that Jesus paid on our behalf. The enemy tries to distract us from accepting Jesus' gift of life. But God's awesome sacrifice has meant hope for all generations, including us today.

> *The enemy tries to distract us from accepting Jesus' gift of life. But God's awesome sacrifice has meant hope for all generations, including us today.*

We are assured that God will not ignore "a broken and a contrite heart" (Ps. 51:17), but God doesn't intend for us to stay broken. Psalm 147:3 tells us that God "healeth the broken in heart." God cannot help us unless we let go of our self-righteousness and accept His righteousness and obey and follow Him.

In John 21:15–17 we read that Peter testified of his love for Jesus, and Jesus instructed Peter to feed His lambs and His sheep. Peter's story does show that people can change from being self-justified to God-justified. Peter went from being violent when he cut off the servant's ear, to being defensive when he was accused of being with Jesus, to being broken when he realized he had denied Jesus, to being free when he accepted God's forgiveness. This restorative process is available to us all.

Different Responses to Accusations

"Who shall lay any thing to the charge of God's elect? It is God that justifieth." Romans 8:33

People respond differently to situations where they are accused. There are many biblical examples of this. For instance, in 2 Samuel 11 we read that David had committed sin, and God sent Nathan the prophet to reveal the grave sin David had committed (see 2 Sam. 12:1–13). Once his sin was revealed, David was convicted of his sin and he did not try to hide his sin or blame others for his wrongdoing.

In 1 Kings 18:17 we read that Ahab the king accused Elijah the prophet of being responsible for Ahab's problems. But Elijah was only revealing the sins that Ahab had committed (1 Kings 18:18). Ahab's exclamation was his attempt to transfer his blame. After standing up to Ahab and the false prophets, when Jezebel, Ahab's wife, entered the picture and declared her intent to see Elijah dead, Elijah fled (1 Kings 19:2, 3). Exhausted, emotionally drained, and tired, Elijah became depressed and wanted to die (1 Kings 19:4). But an angel restored Elijah with something to eat and drink (1 Kings 19:5–7), which gave Elijah enough strength for forty days (1 Kings 19:8). God strengthened and healed Elijah's bruised spirit.

We cannot exhaust the many possibilities, but from these two stories and from the experiences of Peter, Judas, and the two criminals explained previously, we are introduced to:

1. Extreme "blame giver" personality, as seen in Ahab. Ahab sought to transfer blame, even

when there was evidence that he was responsible for the wrong deeds. In this category persons may seek to shift and transfer blame as
much as possible and be overtly defensive.
Persons may shift their arguments as they see
fit. For example, if a "blame giver" tripped over
another's foot, the other person may be told,
"You have no right putting your foot out like
that." And if the other person tripped over the
foot of the "blame giver," he or she may say,
"You should watch where you are going." This
personality may only reluctantly accept blame
when they are unable to hide their wrong.

2. Extreme "blame taker" personality. This personality is consumed with guilt. Since the focus here
is on the end result, this category can also include persons like Judas, who was responsible
for the wrong deeds he had committed. The category can also include persons taking undeserved
blame, who may quickly accept blame even
when there was evidence that they had nothing to do with the problem. Irrespective of how
an individual reaches the extreme "blame taker"
state, this attitude is dangerous because it leads
to an extreme feeling and belief that there is no
hope of ever being forgiven. The extreme attitude
of always taking blame may result from accusations made by others or by self. The "blame taker" would be consumed with guilt for putting his
or her foot in the road to cause another to fall.
Yet if he or she is the one to fall over another's
foot, he or she would be consumed with guilt for
not looking where he or she was going and may

not acknowledge the responsibility others need to take.

3. Rational, objective, and fair personality. These persons will seek the truth and look at things from all angles and objectively critique the situation. They would assess when the situation requires them to blame themselves, to blame others, to share the blame, or even if no one is to blame. Like David, they would accept responsibility for wrong done, and like Elijah, they would honestly state when others should take responsibility for their actions. Peter, who accepted the responsibility for his actions, also experienced guilt, but Peter did not reach the point of drowning in his guilt as described in the "blame taker" category. Even someone striving to keep up a balanced attitude, if confronted over and over by the self-justifying and naturally attacking personality, they might find themselves, over time, becoming exhausted. We see this with Elijah who fled after Jezebel's threats.

Criticism has its place, such as when Jesus critiqued the churches in Revelation 2 and 3 as He sought to restore and heal those who did wrong. Jesus was focused on pruning the character in order for the person to thrive and to grow. But the accusations and verbal attacks where the focus goes from the problem to the

> *The enemy's plan is to condemn us to death, but Jesus paid a high price for us to have life.*

person can threaten to weaken the individual's under-standing of his or her value.

With so many incidences of wrong being committed, with just one measure of doubt, we might be tempted to believe that the accusations we hear are true, and very soon speculation turns to reality in the minds of the hearers. Some blame is legitimate like towards Ahab, but at times the innocent like Elijah are also blamed. The enemy's plan is to condemn us to death, but Jesus paid a high price for us to have life.

The extreme "blame giver" can be led to think that he or she has no need of a Savior. A "blame taker" may feel too unworthy and believe that even a Savior cannot help him or her, but a person with a balanced perspective will accept God and let Him take over his or her life, having acknowledged his or her need of a Savior. Those with balanced personalities will not defend their wrong actions, but with a contrite heart, they will seek God's forgiveness.

This is especially important to understand because the human heart is constantly crying out for justification—it wants to be made right. And we need to avoid trying to make ourselves right on our own. God wants us to allow Him to take over our lives and accept His help in the restorative process. We cannot pay for God's gift of life, but because He has given us so much, we should purpose to accept His forgiveness and walk in His way.

Workplace Interactions

"A word fitly spoken is like apples of gold in pictures of silver." Proverbs 25:11

Since interactions at the workplace occur with peers, bosses, and subordinates, this can almost be described as a kaleidoscope of mixed personalities all working together, with the intent to achieve the company's strategic goals. The psychological byproducts of trying to achieve organizational goals can result in fulfillment for some but distress for others.

When opinions are shared and reactions to opinions occur interchangeably, the focus on the real issue can be lost. The original and primary issue being solved can be clouded by secondary issues because of a shift in focus to the opinions shared and mannerisms displayed by others. This can result in further reactions and hurt feelings among people. The issue is shifted to a personal level.

Sometimes in a conversation, multiple issues emerge with each new issue creating its own conflict. The emergence of more issues and more conflict can reveal that there are other issues that need to be dealt with. The parties would need to have the wisdom and composure to know which issues are trivial and need no further discussion, which issues need to be dealt with in the present conversation, and which issues need to be dealt with at a later date. Sometimes there is the need for either or both parties to apologize and/or accept apologies.

But the aim should be to spend the time to solve the primary problem and keep on track.

Imagine two persons ("Y" and "W") are standing on two different sides of a box, and they can only see their side (see the following figure).

Y's Perspective

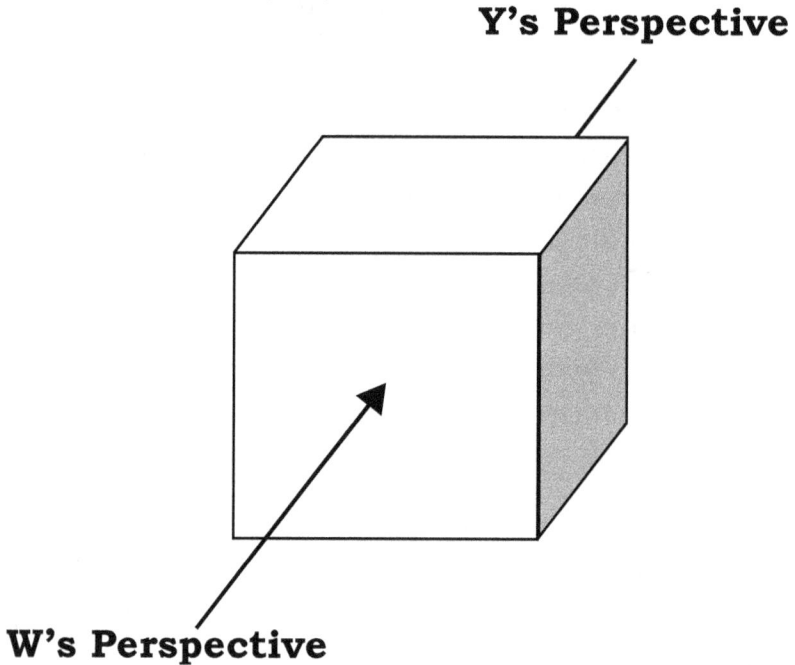

W's Perspective

For Y and W to see what the other can see, they must walk around the box to see the other sides. If we relate this to conversations, this walk around approach (or trying to see things through the eyes of the other) is needed to maintain objectivity, see beyond our side, and stay on track.

Let us consider that Person W was supposed to help a colleague, Person Y, to complete a report by providing critical information by an agreed date ahead of the known report deadline. Person W did not provide the information on time, and Person Y forgot the deadline, so the report was completed very late. Below are possible scenarios with the responses Persons Y and W could give surrounding the problem based on "blame giver," "blame taker," or balanced personalities.

A. **Person W**—blame giver: "You should have reminded me that you needed the information." **Person Y**—blame giver: "You should have remembered to give me the information." Both W and Y would argue and focus on what the other person should have done and focus little or no attention on what they could do collectively so that it does not happen again.

B. **Person W**—blame giver: "You should have reminded me that you needed the information." **Person Y**—balanced: "We could have reminded each other." Person W would argue and try to keep the focus on what Y should have done. However, Y would try to objectively look at things from both sides to see what both parties could do in the future so that it does not happen again.

C. **Person W**—blame giver: "You should have reminded me that you needed the information." **Person Y**—blame taker: "I should have reminded you that I needed the information." In this case, Y would quickly feel fully responsible and focus on what he or she did wrong. Person W would agree with Y and focus on what Y should have done, only adding to Y's mental stress.

D. **Person W**—balanced: "We could have reminded each other." **Person Y**—blame giver: "You should have remembered to give me the information." Person Y would argue and try to keep the focus on what W should have done. Person W would try to objectively look at things from both sides to see what both parties could do in the future so that it does not happen again.

E. **Person W**—balanced: "We could have reminded each other." **Person Y**—balanced: "We could have reminded each other." Both parties would identify the issues truthfully and be able to solve problems with no character attacks. They would both acknowledge the part they could have played to complete the report on time and look to see what could be done so that it does not happen again.

F. **Person W**—balanced: "We could have reminded each other." **Person Y**—blame taker: "I should have reminded you that I needed the information." Person Y would quickly feel fully responsible and focus on what he or she did wrong. Person W would realize that Y is taking unnecessary blame and would not exploit Y's disposition. Hopefully, Y would also look to see what could be done so that it does not happen again.

G. **Person W**—blame taker: "I should have remembered to give you the information." **Person Y**—blame giver: "You should have remembered to give me the information." Person W would quickly feel fully responsible and focus on what he or she did wrong. Person Y would agree with W and focus on what W should have done, only adding to W's mental stress.

H. **Person W**—blame taker: "I should have remembered to give you the information." **Person Y**—balanced: "We could have reminded each other." Person W would quickly feel fully responsible and focus on what he or she did wrong. Person Y would realize that W is taking unnecessary blame and would not exploit W's disposition. Hopefully, W would also look to see what could be done so that it does not happen again.

I. **Person W**—blame taker: "I should have remembered to give you the information." **Person Y**—blame taker: "I should have reminded you that I needed the information." Both W and Y would quickly feel fully responsible and focus primarily on what they individually did wrong, but both may miss the opportunity to collectively find a solution so that it does not happen again.

In scenarios B, C, D, and G, it is evident that the "blame giver" could create and cultivate a stressful situation for the other individual, but scenarios C and G provide examples of even greater human vulnerability of guilt ridden people working with "blame giver" individuals. This can put a lot of strain on much-needed teamwork. There could be incidents where the "blame giver" personality is correct, and there was nothing wrong with what he or she did in a particular situation. But when in the right, the "blame giver" will not readily offer any mercy to the one who is wrong.

In another situation a "blame taker" might be innocent and a "blame giver" is not. The "blame giver" personality may still try to share the blame with the innocent "blame taker" individual.

If we were to add authority to the "blame giver" personality, we can imagine the stress the subordinate will experience when things go wrong. Being a supervisor of a "blame giver" personality would bring some level of stress as well. Maybe some "blame giver" personalities have adopted this approach because they were accused excessively and have now chosen to continue the cycle. They may disregard the opinions of others and feel that they alone have everything to contribute. They may feel that their opinion is always right.

Identifying who is responsible can mean that someone will be held accountable if something goes wrong or receive the affirmation if something goes right. It is easy to take responsibility for the positive and successful things, so when something good happens, people generally are quick to take responsibility. When negative things occur, the "blame giver" will be quick to say someone else is responsible. The focus of the "blame giver" is more on being right and less on solving the problem.

If we were to look at scenario A where both parties are blame givers, the conversation may have them both go as far as saying, "You should have reminded me to remind you." This gives us an idea of the extent that a conversation can become entangled when someone is bent on showing that they are right or not to blame.

The focus of persons Y and W should be on finding the solution to reduce the possible problem the late report could create and to implement measures to avoid repetition of the situation. This is the more important issue, considering the individuals may work together in the future.

Objectively exploring and discussing the possibilities of what should have been done reveals important lessons. These lessons can reveal measures that we can implement to avoid repeating the problem. If managed properly, the exploration can be a beneficial and an enlightening exercise that will highlight:

- the things we are doing well and should continue doing;
- the things we need to improve on and should continue doing;
- the things we should stop doing; and
- the things we should start doing.

With these things in mind, we can build on our experiences for future reference. Even when things go well, it is good to do an assessment to reinforce the good. It is also good to assess the things that worked well in the past, since as circumstances change and team members change, we may need to adjust our approaches to ensure continued success.

Christ provides us with the objectivity we need, and if we humbly ask Him, He will illuminate our minds and broaden our perspectives.

We may shudder at the thought of having a supervisor like Ahab, who did not want to listen to Elijah. Most of us would prefer to work with someone like David. In David's position as king, he listened to Nathan the prophet (see 2 Sam. 12:1–13). Being objective does not mean that there will not be different opinions or perspectives, problems or disagreements. But it is how the parties deal with the issues that will mean the difference between objectivity and biases. The underlying attitude behind our reasoning influences and directs our words and actions.

Christ provides us with the objectivity we need, and if we humbly ask Him, He will illuminate our minds and broaden our perspectives. The balanced attitude would be to acknowledge that someone else's opinions and feelings

are important, your own opinions and feelings are important, so it is possible to work together.

Let us remember, "A man hath joy by the answer of his
mouth: and a word spoken in due season, how good is it!"
(Prov. 15:23). Simple things can escalate into big things,
and understanding the dynamics as summarized in all
the scenarios will help us be aware of the danger zones.
But understanding the dynamics can never replace the
need for the power of God to intervene on our behalf in
our conflicts, since we can only see a part of the picture.
As we face the challenges around us, we need God's guidance to navigate through life. We need to pray continually
for God's strength and discernment and ask God to give
us a balanced and objective attitude.

The Bible is full of stories where Jesus got to the root
of the issues. Today, Jesus will also help us to get to the
root of the issues we face and help us to stay on track. We
need to depend on God, who sees and knows everything.

Jesus came and walked the road, and He knows the
way. Jesus, our High Priest, was "touched with the feeling of our infirmities," and He "was in all points tempted
like as we are, yet without sin" (Heb. 4:15). He is our solution. With God's guidance we will be able to properly assess situations and make intelligent decisions to correctly
deal with every situation.

Section 4:

God's Involvement in Our Lives

Jesus Makes Things Right

"Stand fast therefore in the liberty wherewith Christ hath made us free, and be not entangled again with the yoke of bondage." Galatians 5:1

The Bible records stories of people condemning those who were in need of forgiveness. In Matthew 18:23–34 we read about a servant who owed his master a large amount of money. After the servant pleaded with his master, his master "was moved with compassion, and loosed him, and forgave him the debt" (Matt. 18:27). The forgiven servant then found one of his fellow servants who owed him money, and he demanded that the servant repay the debt. He ignored his fellow servant's pleas for mercy. The debt of this servant was small compared to the debt the forgiven servant had owed. When the master heard, he demanded that the ungrateful servant be punished and repay all. The servant who received forgiveness did not forgive his fellow servant.

In John 8:3–11 we read of accusers who brought a woman caught in adultery to Jesus and challenged Jesus to condemn her. She could not have committed adultery alone, but she was condemned alone. The accusers told Jesus that the sentence for her sin was that she should be stoned. She must have braced herself waiting to feel the first stone on her back. After Jesus wrote on the ground, He said, "He that is without sin among you, let him first cast a stone at her" (John 8:7). Jesus continued to write on the ground. The accusers were "convicted by their own conscience" (John 8:9) and left.

Jesus was the only One who fit the description of being sinless, and He did not hurl a stone. Instead, Jesus provided healing. Instead of meeting condemnation, the accused met a Savior. Jesus spoke kindly to the woman and asked her, "Woman, where are those thine accusers? hath no man condemned thee?" (John 8:10). And she replied, "No man, Lord" (John 8:11). Then she heard the most comforting words any repentant guilty person could hear, "Neither do I condemn thee; go, and sin no more" (John 8:11).

Jesus' action is a wonderful display of not condoning wrong but possessing tender care for the wrongdoer. God provides hope in otherwise hopeless situations. The accused was left free and forgiven of her sins while the accusers left the scene, still in their sins.

If we contrast the ungrateful servant's attitude to Jesus' treatment of the woman caught in adultery, we see the sinful one condemning and the Sinless One forgiving. The ungrateful servant was forgiven for more than he was willing to forgive another. Because of the ungrateful servant's condemning and accusing attitude, he inflicted pain on the other servant, and sadly, the ungrateful servant did not experience healing.

Some people may try to defend themselves and use persuasive arguments to convince fellow human beings (who are unable to see the big picture) to believe their side of the story. At times, the guilty are freed because their articulate arguments free them in the minds of the hearers, and the innocent are condemned because their words fall short of convincing others of their innocence. These instances may cause us to struggle and become tired of our fallen world. We long to be rid of sin and wish to fully enjoy God's perfect system of love, justice, grace, and mercy. But the Bible assures us that God is addressing the sin problem.

One part of the solution to sin is that when we approach God in prayer, we are approaching the sinless, all-knowing God, who can read the thoughts and intent of the heart and knows everything we have ever done. God knows who is guilty and who is innocent, so we can always take comfort in the fact that God knows the truth.

Another part of the solution is that God brings awareness of the issues and puts them in the context of the bigger controversy. Jesus alone can help us to face the wrong in ourselves and in others without getting into the accusing cycle. However, God's restorative process to make things right never condones sin, so we should never try to reason wrong away; wrongs committed always deserve to be punished. We see the consequences of wrong every day, and thankfully, Jesus' death provides the final part of the solution to sin so that we will not have to experience eternal death and separation from God.

> *Knowing that Jesus justifies us, we are mentally free to spend all our time learning of God and obeying His Word.*

Psalm 66:18 says, "If I regard iniquity in my heart, the Lord will not hear me," and Matthew 24:12 states, "And because iniquity shall abound, the love of many shall wax cold." From these verses we understand that sin in our hearts will hinder our communication with God and cripple our relationships with each other. But because the "iniquity of us all" (Isa. 53:6) was laid on Jesus, Jesus has made provisions for us all to experience forgiveness, and He wants to replace each "stony heart" with a "heart of flesh" (Ezek. 36:26).

Jesus wants us to bring every broken, guilt-filled attitude to Him to be cleaned up. Jesus wants us to bring every harmful, critical, accusing, and condemning attitude to Him to be cleaned up. Jesus wants us to accept His sacrifice so "that he might redeem us from all iniquity, and purify unto himself a peculiar people, zealous of good works" (Titus 2:14). God provides us with the power to live "and sin no more" (John 8:11). Deliverance from sin is reflected in the desire to obey God's Word. It is liberating to know that we do not have to walk around being and feeling condemned, guilty, and angry.

Knowing that Jesus justifies us, we are mentally free to spend all our time learning of God and obeying His Word. No longer entangled by what others say of us or trapped by the urge to respond to every accusation, we focus on what God says of us. We focus on being whole in Christ. Like His encouraging words to the woman caught in adultery, Jesus encourages us, supports us, and wishes for our happiness in Him, our Creator. Only Jesus can make things right in our lives; only He can save us from the stones of our accusers.

Let us follow Jesus' example and display care and thoughtfulness in our words and actions. The rippling effect will allow love to reach beyond the one to whom it was directly shown, as the recipients of kindness in turn share love with others. With a smile, a kind word, or a gentle touch, we can help to brighten the lives of those with whom we meet. Let us use each occasion to reflect God's light and sow seeds of kindness.

Staying Connected to the Vine

"Brethren, I count not myself to have apprehend-
ed: but this one thing I do, forgetting those things
which are behind, and reaching forth unto those
things which are before, I press toward the mark
for the prize of the high calling of God in Christ
Jesus." Philippians 3:13, 14

Sin has created problems and challenges for every human being, so we will face difficult situations that could involve accusations of some sort. We have already explored the reality that people can be accused and condemned by themselves or by others. Though the person being condemned may be guilty, the person seeking to expose the wrong could have a right or wrong attitude.

In Ephesians 4:15 we are advised to speak "the truth in love," so when dealing with delicate and difficult situations, we need to be conscious of our attitude. As we interact with others, we should focus on helping each other positively along the path of life. Sometimes this is easier said than done.

The story of Job provides a good example of how persons who mean well can inflict emotional pain on their loved ones. Job's friends came to him with the wrong attitude. Though they visited him with the objective "to mourn with him and to comfort him" (Job 2:11), when they began to speak, they spoke in condemnation. Job was innocent of the charges his friends laid against him, and Job told his friends that they should have kept silent (Job 13:5). In Job 42:10 we read that as part of the healing for Job, he forgave his friends.

However, Job had an exceptional character. It is understandable that some people may struggle to overcome bitterness and anger if they were wrongfully accused. They may find it difficult to forgive those who have marred their character, but clinging to an attitude of bitterness can cause many people emotional pain. In addition, for those we approach who have committed wrong, they may feel so hopeless that it could result in them being consumed by guilt, consequently causing the belief that they cannot be forgiven. It is with this in mind that we should precede with caution when approaching a person with an accusation.

Another attitude a person could have may lead them to accept they are wrong but with no remorse. In other cases, guilty people may reject the accusations irrespective of whether or not the person bringing the issues to their attention has the right or wrong attitude. The accused persons may even seek to blame others.

It is difficult, at times, to discern what we should say and what we should not say to those we feel may need our guidance. It is not only a time to pray for the individual we are considering to approach, but it is also a time to pray for ourselves, as only God's wisdom will provide aid in delicate situations. The most important thing is to reach out and cling to Jesus for support, and He will work through us to better help others.

The story of the woman with the issue of blood is a good example of determination to reach and connect to Jesus. Through the noise and the crowds, the woman kept focused on Jesus. She was not distracted, but as she pressed closer, she touched Jesus' garment and received healing (Mark 5:24–29). Amidst the distractions, we must also reach out in faith and touch Jesus' garments each day. Jesus will recognize our touch of faith, and He will respond to our concerns.

If we cling to Jesus and His Word then we will find the way to say what is needed to those who need to hear it. If all goes well, the guilty persons may accept they are wrong with an attitude to seek forgiveness. First John 2:1, 2 records, "These things write I unto you, that ye sin not. And if any man sin, we have an advocate with the Father, Jesus Christ the righteous: And he is the propitiation for our sins: and not for ours only, but also for the sins of the whole world." It is wonderful to know that we have an avenue through Jesus to seek and receive God's forgiveness, and hopefully the accused will understand this and rejoice in it. We also need to ask God to give us the humility to address the wrongs we have committed that others bring to our attention.

Jesus gave us the example of connecting to God and constantly drawing strength from our heavenly Father. We need to commune with Him daily in prayer for guidance, discernment, and wisdom, especially when communicating with others. We need to daily read and soak our minds in God's Word, so we can live His Word. In Psalm 119:11 we read, "Thy word have I hid in mine heart, that I might not sin against thee." God's Word hidden in our hearts will aid us to obey Him.

Therefore, for us to follow Jesus' example, we must have God's Word stored in our hearts before the battle begins. And Jeremiah 15:16 states, "Thy words were found, and I did eat them; and thy word was unto me the joy and rejoicing of mine heart: for I am called by thy name, O Lord God of hosts." We also need to listen to God's response to us. This is the same as when a child follows his or her parent. The child must keep his or her eyes on the parent at all times. The child also learns to recognize his or her parent's voice.

In John 10:27, 28 Jesus tells us, "My sheep hear my voice, and I know them, and they follow me: And I give unto them eternal life; and they shall never perish, neither shall any man pluck them out of my hand." In John 10:14 we read, "I am the good shepherd, and know my sheep, and am known of mine." Jesus knows His people, and they, in turn, know His voice and follow Him. It becomes a two-way relationship. So instead of being a part of an accusing cycle, we now become a part of a communion and obedience cycle with Christ. Enoch and Noah knew the joy of that communion (Gen. 5:22–24; Gen. 6:9), a communion that we learn more about each day.

> *With God's help each decision and response we make to the issues we face can represent a step towards reflecting God's image.*

If a laptop computer is unplugged, we may continue working until we see the sign on the screen that signals a low battery: "You should charge your battery or switch to outlet power to keep from losing your work." We cannot live without God, the life-giver, and we need not wait to get a "low battery" warning to decide to connect to God. We need to be connected all the time. Thinking we are connected is not enough. We need to be sure. Acts 17:28 says, "For in him we live, and move, and have our being; ... For we are also his offspring." It does not matter how much knowledge we have stored in our memories, we cannot live without the Source of life, without the connection to God.

When we are connected to God, the Holy Spirit puts our thoughts in the correct perspective. He reminds us of

Bible truths stored in our mind, and He provides us with insight from similar challenges faced by God's people in the Bible. Jesus brings things into perspective and keeps our focus on important things. With God's help each decision and response we make to the issues we face can represent a step towards reflecting God's image. So when we need to decide how we will treat or communicate with another person, the Holy Spirit will remind us that we are reaching for God's standard.

When our eyes are completely and firmly fixed on Jesus, we are connected to God, and God's love will flow through us to others. We will be sensitive to the cries of others. Jesus will direct His obedient children to work in the restorative process for others. When we rise to face the daily activities of life after spending time with Jesus, our conversations and actions will show that we have been with God. Let us encourage each other to continue pressing towards God's mark.

Section 5:

Our Growth

Beauty for Ashes

"But the fruit of the Spirit is love, joy, peace, long-suffering, gentleness, goodness, faith, meekness, temperance: against such there is no law."
Galatians 5:22, 23

Having accepted Jesus' way, and having experienced God's healing and the leading of the Holy Spirit, we become fruitful. We stay with and abide in Christ (John 15:5). Though we may be surrounded by negativity, discouragement, and hopelessness, the good news is that we are being nourished when we study the Bible and pray continually. We draw our spiritual nutrients from the Holy Spirit, and the fruit of the Spirit will be the evidence that God is working in our lives. The Bible also tells us that the person who meditates on God's law "day and night ... shall be like a tree planted by the rivers of water, that bringeth forth his fruit in his season" (Ps. 1:2, 3).

> *We draw our spiritual nutrients from the Holy Spirit, and the fruit of the Spirit will be the evidence that God is working in our lives.*

"The works of the flesh" (Gal. 5:19–21) oppose the fruit of the Spirit. John 10:10 tells us, "The thief cometh not, but for to steal, and to kill, and to destroy." However, this verse also tells us that Jesus came so that we would "have life, and ... have it more abundantly." Knowing that "greater is he that is in you, than he that is in the world" (1 John 4:4), we are reassured that the Holy Spirit's work in us allows us to live the victorious Christian life, and we are moved in a positive direction. We rely on and experience God's overcoming power. Jesus gives us "beauty for ashes, the oil of joy for mourning, the garment of praise for the spirit of heaviness; that [we] might be called trees of righteousness, the planting of the LORD, that he might be glorified" (Isa. 61:3). Only in Jesus can we receive something of infinite more value than what we can afford.

As God continues the transforming process in our lives and we are brought under His subjection, the process of exchanging our works of the flesh for His fruit continues until only the fruit of the Holy Spirit is radiating in us. We will continue to "grow in grace, and in the knowledge of our Lord and Saviour Jesus Christ" (2 Peter 3:18). The Holy Spirit produces fruit in us that is a blessing to everyone around us, including ourselves.

We can view the fruit of the Spirit, "love, joy, peace, longsuffering, gentleness, goodness, faith, meekness, temperance" (Gal. 5:22, 23), as a rope with nine cords that create a strong bond between God and us. The works of the flesh would leave us in a "horrible pit," but as we hold onto the rope, Jesus is pulling us out of the "miry clay," and He is setting our "feet upon a rock" (Ps. 40:2).

Paul tells us in Galatians 2:20, "I am crucified with Christ: nevertheless I live; yet not I, but Christ liveth in me: and the life which I now live in the flesh I live by the faith of the Son of God, who loved me, and gave himself for me." The fruit of the Spirit in us is the result of our death to self and embracing life in Christ.

Love

*"Beloved, let us love one another: for love is of
God; and every one that loveth is born of God,
and knoweth God. He that loveth not knoweth not
God; for God is love." 1 John 4:7, 8*

God's love heals us from the pain of bad experiences, broken relationships, and broken promises. God's love changes us and causes us to grow. As Paul told us, nothing "shall be able to separate us from the love of God, which is in Christ Jesus our Lord" (Rom. 8:39). Second Timothy 1:7 tells us, "God hath not given us the spirit of fear; but of power, and of love, and of a sound mind." When we experience God's love, we lose all fear and bitterness and choose to take up His characteristics instead. It is a revolutionary, life-changing process. As Paul told us, nothing can separate us from God's love, and if we nurture His love inside our hearts, we cannot help but be changed by it.

First John 3:1 tells us, "Behold, what manner of love the Father hath bestowed upon us, that we should be called the sons of God." First Corinthians 13:4, 5 tells us that charity or love "is not puffed up ... [and] seeketh not her own." It is only possible to live this description of love if God's love fills us and is the motivation behind our actions. As we grow in Christ, God's love becomes more evident in us, and as we read God's Word and internalize what He did for us, our vision of Christ will become clearer.

One aspect of His love is described in 2 Corinthians 5:14 where we read, "For the love of Christ constraineth us." Joseph understood this, and his love for God propelled him in the midst of temptation to say, "How then can I do this great wickedness, and sin against God?" (Gen. 39:9). Joseph fled from the place of temptation instead of staying and doing wrong. Joseph acknowledged that he did not live for himself; he lived for God. Thankfully, our Creator's love for us is all consuming, and we are able to experience His love for us when we do right as well as when we do wrong.

Acknowledging how our actions affect others, we will want to make things right with those whom we may have wronged.

Another feature of God's love in us is that it gives us a different perspective on the wrongs we may have ignored or may have felt justified to do. We are not only concerned about our own welfare and well-being but also about the welfare and well-being of others. We realize that our actions do matter. Acknowledging how our actions affect others, we will want to make things right with those whom we may have wronged. This is shown in the life of Zacchaeus (Luke 19:1–10). When Zacchaeus experienced Jesus' forgiveness and healing, he realized his responsibility to help mend broken relationships. Zacchaeus acknowledged he had hurt others and sought to do all he could to stop the negative consequences of his actions. In Luke 19:8 we read that Zacchaeus said, "If I have taken any thing from any man by false accusation, I restore him fourfold." Zacchaeus got involved in the restoration process found only by experiencing God's love.

In life the negative results of wrong cannot always be halted. Sometimes because of the nature of the wrong, restoration does not occur, but Zacchaeus' story does show that when we experience and embrace God's love, our hearts will be changed, and we will desire to make amends with each other when possible. We will feel the difference in our hearts, and those around us will also notice the change only love can bring.

Joy

"The joy of the LORD is your strength."
Nehemiah 8:10

We all need strength. Even if we know the right thing to do, we still need the strength to do it. Joy affects, influences, and determines our attitude. Proverbs 17:22 says, "A merry heart doeth good like a medicine: but a broken spirit drieth the bones." Our attitude can wear us down or lift us up. If we live God's way, we feel God's joy, which replaces the bitterness and guilt.

Being joyful doesn't mean that we like or accept the ills that happen around us, nor does being joyful mean that we will ignore the sufferings that occur and live isolated and unaware of the pain around us. Joy acknowledges the hand of God and His involvement in our lives and the lives of others, and joy reassures us that we are not going through difficulties alone. Because we are assured that God has everything under control, we can be joyful. Joy ties in with faith.

Imagine a child hiding behind a bigger sibling, who defends the child from a bully. That child feels joy knowing the problem is not his or hers alone to face. We have the joy of knowing Jesus' sacrifice means the gift of salvation is available to every human being.

We are also told that "weeping may endure for a night, but joy cometh in the morning" (Ps. 30:5). David in his grief and guilt asked for the joy of God's salvation to be restored to him (Ps. 51:12). His guilt had caused him to lose the joy he knew in happier times. In Matthew 9:2 Jesus said to the sick man, "be of good cheer; thy sins be forgiven thee." We would be in despair without Christ, but with Jesus there's the conviction that God "hath made every thing beautiful in his time" (Eccles. 3:11).

Jesus gives us "the oil of joy for mourning" (Isa. 61:3). He wants His joy to remain in us and our joy to be full (John 15:11), and we can rest in that assurance. The joy Jesus gives us will be seen in our countenance and will radiate outward. Psalm 16:11 states, "in [God's] presence is fulness of joy." Our sustained joy comes from accepting Jesus' salvation and staying connected to Him.

Peace

*"Thou wilt keep him in perfect peace, whose mind
is stayed on thee: because he trusteth in thee."*
Isaiah 26:3

In Romans 7:14–25 Paul explains the spiritual wrestling that we experience to overcome sin as we continue to grow in Christ; he brings to light the struggle we go through to do what is right and say no to wrong. This battle continues as long as we walk our spiritual path. As the Holy Spirit reveals to us the areas in our lives that are contrary to His will, the Holy Spirit will also prompt us to submit these areas to Him so that we may overcome.

Because Jesus covers us with His "robe of righteousness" and we no longer experience condemnation and separation, we find peace.

When we realize we need to be changed as we continue to "press toward the mark" (Phil. 3:14), we may be tempted to feel that we have lost the peace of God. But we must always remember that the enemy continually seeks to inflict emotional torment. He wants to use our sins as reasons for us to be destroyed (see Rev. 12:10), and he will seek to accuse us and remind us of our past sins and of our present imperfections.

Mental torment can be seen as the opposite of peace. Guilt erodes our peace. The fear of the consequences of wrong acts can affect our ability to relax. We are not to ignore our sins; instead, we should confess them. "If we confess our sins, [God] is faithful and just to forgive us our sins, and to cleanse us from all unrighteousness" (1 John 1:9). Then because Jesus covers us with His "robe of righteousness" (Isa. 61:10) and we no longer experience condemnation and separation, we find peace.

We also are told, however, that we should not pretend to experience peace when peace doesn't exist (Jer. 6:14; Ezek. 13:10). Peace is not being numb, but peace comes as a result of having experienced Jesus' healing touch. If we take "the gospel of peace" (Eph. 6:15), we share God's message with whom we interact. Psalm 119:165 tells us, "Great peace have they which love thy law: and nothing shall offend them." We are to love and obey God's law. Though we are not saved by what we do, disobedience to God's law is evidence that God is not leading our lives. Without God's guidance, we cannot obtain true peace. If we submit to His will, we will be glad in the comfort His peace brings us.

Like joy, this inner attitude of peace will emit outward. We are encouraged to "be at peace among" each other (1 Thess. 5:13) and to "follow peace with all men" (Heb. 12:14). We are to "seek peace, and pursue it" (Ps. 34:14) and "if it be possible ... live peaceably with all men" (Rom. 12:18). "The peace of God, which passeth all understanding, shall keep [our] hearts and minds through Christ Jesus" (Phil. 4:7). In Proverbs 3:5, 6 we are told to "trust in the LORD with all thine heart; and lean not unto thine own understanding. In all thy ways acknowledge him, and he shall direct thy paths." This is a powerful promise and beautifully describes the Christian journey. Having peace and trust in God are interwoven. If we trust in God, we will experience God's peace. Jesus' peace will fill us and surround us.

As the disciples were in the boat and the seas became rough, their peace was eroded, and they became afraid. Jesus asked them, "Why are ye fearful, O ye of little faith?" (Matt. 8:26). In Luke 21:26 we are told about "men's hearts failing them for fear." This Bible verse shows us what the absence of peace can do to an individual and highlights the value of peace to maintain our lives. God tells us, "Fear thou not; for I am with thee: be not dismayed; for I am thy God: I will strengthen thee; yea, I will help thee; yea, I will uphold thee with the right hand of my righteousness" (Isa. 41:10).

There is only one type of fear we need to have. Proverbs 9:10 tells us that "the fear of the LORD is the beginning of wisdom." This fear gives respect and reverence to Jesus. This fear brings us into the presence of our awesome God and gives us the true perspective about life and who we are. In Psalm 34:4 we read, "I sought the LORD, and he heard me, and delivered me from all my fears." We are reassured that we don't have to live in torment; if we come to God in faith and ask Him, God will give us peace.

Longsuffering

"Now the God of patience and consolation grant you to be likeminded one toward another according to Christ Jesus." Romans 15:5

We may have witnessed two persons speaking together quietly at first. We may have heard them raise their voices and raise their hands with clenched fists. We may then have seen punches follow and things thrown across a room. We may have seen persons who were wronged take matters into their own hands. Many times the focus and blame shift from the initial wrong to the secondary wrong. After the event we may have heard the persons grieving that they were unable to control their tempers, especially if they have to face negative consequences as a result of their decisions.

Impulsive actions can result in the loss of future happiness because of the consequences of the thoughtless actions, and the downward spiral can continue. To be longsuffering is a very important attribute if we are to achieve healthy relationships and personal development. We are told, "A wrathful man stirreth up strife: but he that is slow to anger appeaseth strife" (Prov. 15:18). This tells us that we should always be longsuffering and not be quick to lose our tempers, even if provoked. It is important to consider the things that can increase our vulnerability when we are provoked. Factors like poor eating habits and even lack of sleep can cause us to react negatively to situations that may have otherwise seemed trivial.

To prevent pressure build-up in equipment during operation, pressure relief valves are installed to release the pressure before the pressure level can damage the equipment or the people around. Similarly, sometimes situations can make it difficult for us to remain calm, especially when we repeatedly go through the same struggles. We need to find ways to moderate the stress we experience so that we can continue being positive and constructive. David also experienced a desire to get away from challenges. In Psalm 55:6 we read, "Oh that I had wings like a dove! for then would I fly away, and be at rest."

> *Maintaining the hope that we will experience future joy helps us to be longsuffering and patient.*

Maintaining the hope that we will experience future joy helps us to be longsuffering and patient. We see this trait displayed in persons working towards a cherished goal: students willing to put in extra hours of preparation in order to pass an exam, or musicians who spend long hours perfecting their skill. Longsuffering requires stamina, stick-to-itiveness, holding on until the end and not giving up.

First Corinthians 13:4 tells us that "charity suffereth long." This verse gives us a good example of the interconnectivity of the components of the fruit of the Holy Spirit. Love is a very important ingredient that helps to increase our tolerance—not tolerance for injustice but tolerance to wait when required to let the good seed grow. This attribute is also displayed when persons are willing to sacrifice for the benefit of others, for example, lovingly taking care of the sick over an extended period of time.

But longsuffering is also the attitude we must have in the midst of experiences beyond our control. If we are confident of God's leading, we can rest in His love and "wait patiently for him" (Ps. 37:7). Being longsuffering means thinking before acting and waiting to hear God's voice to know when we are to move. Sometimes His voice comes when we least expect it, and sometimes God waits a long time to tell us what to do.

When we are waiting for an answer from God, being longsuffering isn't always easy. The word "suffering" tells us that the experience or situation in which we presently find ourselves is not where we want to be nor what we enjoy. However, we should keep in mind that the experience may be important for some future benefit or good. We will not naturally gravitate to or look forward to suffering because it is something we would be relieved to get behind us, yet in the Christian walk, it is a part of the package— it is an attribute that helps to develop our character. In 1 Peter 1:6 and 7, we read, "Wherein ye greatly rejoice, though now for a season, if need be, ye are in heaviness through manifold temptations: That the trial of your faith, being much more precious than of gold that perisheth, though it be tried with fire, might be found unto praise and honour and glory at the appearing of Jesus Christ." The challenge is to experience joy and peace in our hearts during such times, or even love towards those who have caused us pain.

Sometimes we may feel that we are on a treadmill in our existence. We are running, yet when we look around, we see the same scenes. During these times we may feel we are not growing or that we are going nowhere. Although we are trying to follow God's leading as best as we can, we may feel stagnated and that we are living below our human potential. But during these times we are building stamina. Amidst the disappointments there are lessons to be learned.

Longsuffering does not mean staying in a volatile and provoking situation or tolerating or accepting everything. The Bible says we are to "abstain from all appearance of evil" (1 Thess. 5:22), and this includes removing ourselves, where possible, from provoking and unhealthy situations. Jesus never accepted the disrespect shown by the moneychangers in His Father's house (Matt. 21:12, 13), but He showed tolerance and patience on the cross carrying the sins of the world. He said, "Father, forgive them; for they know not what they do" (Luke 23:34).

In every situation we need to be aware of when God is directing us to another stage. And as we stay connected to God, we will depend on Him to subside any fear of the unknown and give us the strength to move on from our current position to the place He is directing us to go. At each stage of our growth, being longsuffering is to be a part of our Christian response to God's leading.

Gentleness

"And the servant of the Lord must not strive; but
be gentle unto all men, apt to teach, patient."
2 Timothy 2:24

When we hear "gentleness," we think of someone who is not harsh. Gentleness describes a particular manner of approaching situations in life. It is kindness and tenderness that seeks to heal, restore, and edify others. There is no greater example of gentleness than that which is found in Jesus.

Jesus is seen calling the children to Him, taking "them up in his arms" and blessing them (see Mark 10:14–16). Jesus showed gentleness to the woman at the well (John 4:13, 14), the woman caught in adultery (John 8:11), and the woman with the issue of blood (Matt. 9:22; Luke 8:48). There was no threat to the individual in Jesus' gentle approach. Jesus reassured them as people of worth, and they felt Jesus' security.

David also showed a spirit of gentleness in his approach to Jonathan's son. Mephibosheth was afraid that the king wanted to kill him because he was the grandson of Saul, but when he approached David, Mephibosheth realized he had nothing to fear (see 2 Sam. 9:6–8).

We are to be gentle with others, since we have experienced the gentleness of a merciful God. God, instead of giving us what we deserved, softly calls us to Him, and we can confidently call Him, "Abba, Father" (Rom. 8:15; Gal. 4:6). We have many opportunities to display this attribute of gentleness, like when we are dealing with others who may be vulnerable or when it is time to exert authority over others. This is reflected in Isaiah 40:11.

The shepherd gently leads his sheep. He is conscious of their vulnerability and will do nothing to cause the sheep hurt or pain.

Proverbs 15:1 says, "A soft answer turneth away wrath: but grievous words stir up anger." Displaying a gentle personality will mean that we try to avoid provoking others. Gentleness bridges gaps in relationships, and it helps people to avoid unnecessary contention and strife. In 1 Thessalonians 2:7 Paul compares the gentleness shown by himself and his fellow workers to the gentleness of a nurse with her children. Being gentle does not mean compromising standards or condoning wrong, but the spirit of gentleness says we respect each other as God's children even when we need to be firm. Gentleness allows

> *Gentleness bridges gaps in relationships, and it helps people to avoid unnecessary contention and strife.*

us to be able to speak "the truth in love" (Eph. 4:15). Let us pray each day that gentleness remains in our hearts.

Goodness

*"Providing for honest things, not only in the sight
of the Lord, but also in the sight of men."*
2 Corinthians 8:21

The Bible says, "Every good gift and every perfect gift is from above, and cometh down from the Father of lights" (James 1:17); therefore, goodness can only come from God. Psalm 52:1 says, "The goodness of God endureth continually." God's goodness is everlasting, and we cannot truly obtain it unless we develop a relationship with Him.

Paul understood that to be good was not achieved with good intentions. He said, "For I know that in me (that is, in my flesh,) dwelleth no good thing: for to will is present with me; but how to perform that which is good I find not. For the good that I would I do not: but the evil which I would not, that I do" (Rom. 7:18, 19). The good we do is only the result of the Holy Spirit working in us. As we submit to God, His goodness is reflected through us, so God must receive all the glory for all the good done through us.

Through the Holy Spirit's transforming power, the goodness rooted in our hearts will reflect in who we are, what we stand for, and the actions we commit. God expects us to consider others in whatever we do. When we relate to others, we are to combine a gentle spirit with good deeds. We can expect that goodness will show itself in what we do and how we do it.

We are to "ever follow that which is good" (1 Thess. 5:15). "The fear of the LORD is to hate evil" (Prov. 8:13). Goodness is associated with virtues, and it involves maintaining honesty and integrity. We hear things about other people such as whether or not he or she is a good or honest person. People will try to determine whether or not other people have integrity or if they honor their word. In the world today where the pressure exists to compromise, goodness is critical. We have seen what happens when goodness is lacking.

In Hebrews 13:18 we read, "For we trust we have a good conscience, in all things willing to live honestly." Goodness involves doing the right thing and refraining from doing wrong or bad things, even if we believe that no one will see or notice our actions. We should submit to the Holy Spirit's leading to do good even if there is no reward. The good act done is not motivated because of the consequences but because the action is right and it is what God requires of us. If we have respect for God and accept His standard, we will reflect God's values in our actions.

When the Holy Spirit is in charge of our lives, we will desire to do good deeds and take care of what we can for the benefit of others. In Luke 10:33–35 we read of the good deeds of the Samaritan, who saw a wounded man and "had compassion on him" and helped him. The Samaritan did not help because he expected to receive a reward in the future. Seeds of goodness will bear fruit, even if it is for another person's benefit.

Philippians 4:8 states, "Whatsoever things are true, ... honest, ... just, ... pure, ... lovely, ... of good report; if there be any virtue, and if there be any praise, [we are to] think on these things." In Psalm 119:37 the psalmist said, "Turn away mine eyes from beholding vanity; and quicken thou me in thy way." The psalmist understood that not only did he need God to help him to turn away from negative influences but he also needed God to lead him in the right way.

Second Corinthians 3:18 tells us, "We all, with open face beholding as in a glass the glory of the Lord, are changed into the same image from glory to glory." As we expose our minds to things with virtue and all things that are good, we will be influenced positively and ultimately better influence the world.

Faith

"Now faith is the substance of things hoped for,
the evidence of things not seen." Hebrews 11:1

It is interesting for faith to be associated with substance because substance refers to something with body and depth that can be held or felt. Evidence suggests that there are facts and a physical manifestation supporting the theory or belief one is trying to prove.

Anyone who walks into a restaurant knows there are exciting recipes being prepared in the kitchen, even before seeing the food brought to the table. This is because of the aroma. If the individual is hungry, then he or she will have an even greater level of anticipation regarding what is to come. In a similar way, there are many things around us that show or prove God's involvement in our lives, and He uses these things to help us to learn to trust Him more. Faith reinforces that God is providing us with the security we are all yearning for. Opportunities placed in our way also show how God is involved in our lives. It is through the daily "substance" and evidence that God reveals how He is working on our behalf.

Faith says, "I believe God will do what He says He will do." Faith acknowledges we can't see everything, but during times of doubt, faith leads us to trust the One who sees and knows everything. Faith reassures us that God knows what He is doing, even if we feel lost. Faith keeps us aware of God's presence in our lives. For instance, if we are traveling around a bend, we follow the road and keep to our side, confident the road continues even though we can't see the entire road all at once. Through faith we keep traveling on God's side, and we continue believing and trusting that He will take care of us on our journey.

Once as I was boarding an aircraft, I saw some thick black clouds and was uncertain as to whether the pilot was going to be able to fly through those clouds. Before the aircraft took off, there was a heavy downpour, and the ground staff headed for the building, while we the passengers and the crew remained on the airplane. It was a small airplane, so there was no jet bridge to lead us back to the terminal. For about an hour, the water pelted down on the airplane, and because of the heavy winds, we felt the airplane rock from side to side. When it was all over, we got off the airplane, and the maintenance personnel inspected the airplane. About three hours later we boarded the airplane again and were told that the airplane had to get additional fuel. It seemed the flight plan had changed.

I needed faith because I didn't see the checks performed by the maintenance personnel, neither did I see when the refueling of the airplane was done. I didn't see all the preparations that went into ensuring that the airplane would fly safely to its destination. The trust I was placing in the flight staff reminded me of the trust I need to have in God, who is guiding us home, and who provides us with peace and hope while we submit to Him in love, even in the face of a storm.

As Christians, we are confident that Jesus came to this earth to redeem us. He paved the way and left a map to direct us to our heavenly home. Sometimes there are turbulences, but we can depend on the Holy Spirit to take us safely to our destination. Faith provides assurance for the future, but fearing the unknown can erode our peace and create restlessness in our hearts. This restlessness can cause us to act impatiently in order to protect ourselves from some perceived future ill fate.

Absence of faith in God's provision could affect us so that we fail to be kind and to display goodness to others. Lack of faith can also cause persons to feel they must try to do for themselves what they should rely on God to do for them. Faith in God shows God's love has been made complete in us. It reveals that we are not trying to control our lives on our own.

The Bible says, "Faith without works is dead" (James 2:20, 26). If those who have a test choose to be temperate and disciplined and study consistently before the exam, the students can then rest peacefully the night before and be confident that the Holy Spirit will bring back to mind what they need to know. Faith encourages us to try with vigor and drive, to exercise patience, and to wisely manage our resources and time. Faith produces action directed by the Holy Spirit.

The focus here is not on misapplied confidence or misguided optimism or even a self-sufficient attitude. The focus is on an attitude that accepts our human helplessness, our hopeless conditions, our inability to save ourselves, and our need to totally depend on and trust in Jesus. Faith is not trying to maintain a belief or convince ourselves that Jesus will do the things we want Him to do for us. Faith is a yielding of ourselves to Him as we become fully committed to understanding His will for our lives. When we believe His way is best, we allow the Holy Spirit to transform our thinking to become in line with the mind of Christ. Faith is not focused on what we want to get from God but directs us to seek to be like Jesus and openly and objectively meet Him on His terms.

The Bible says in Ephesians 6:11 that we are to "put on the whole armour of God," and we are to take "the shield of faith" (Eph. 6:16). The shield of faith not only protects us from the darts of doubt that question God's creative authority but the shield also protects us from the darts of doubt that can confuse and cloud our decision making process. Imbedded in faith is hope (see Heb. 11:1). In 1 Thessalonians 5:8 we are advised to put "on the breastplate of faith and love; and for an helmet, the hope of salvation." Second Thessalonians 1:3 tells us that faith has the ability to grow exceedingly. Ephesians 2:8, 9 says, "For by grace are ye saved through faith; and that not of yourselves: it is the gift of God: Not of works, lest any man should boast." First Peter 1:5 says that we "are kept by the power of God through faith unto salvation." Faith is the conduit through which we are saved because faith and salvation are connected. By faith, we believe that our new life in Christ starts now.

> *Faith is the conduit through which we are saved because faith and salvation are connected. By faith, we believe that our new life in Christ starts now.*

Despite the many positive effects of living by faith, because of circumstances, we may, at times, feel alone, but we can gain comfort knowing that others have stood up for their faith as well. There are other people in the world, who we may not meet before we reach heaven, who continue to "fight the good fight of faith" (1 Tim. 6:12). They, like us, have also determined to stand for God, and we, the many overcomers and faith travelers, will all one day meet in heaven! What a wonderful gathering and meeting that will be for us all.

Meekness

"Blessed are the meek: for they shall inherit the earth." Matthew 5:5

Meekness constantly reminds us that we can do nothing without Jesus (see John 15:5). We accept that we are to "worship and bow down ... [and to] kneel before the LORD our maker" (Ps. 95:6). We acknowledge our complete dependence on God and our need to submit completely to His leading.

In the absence of meekness, we no longer depend on God. Sadly, we would depend on ourselves and our own abilities. Second Chronicles 7:14 tells us, "If my people, which are called by my name, shall humble themselves, and pray, and seek my face, and turn from their wicked ways; then will I hear from heaven, and will forgive their sin, and will heal their land." Being meek is a reminder that we are not in control and that there is Someone bigger, wiser, and stronger than us. Thankfully, we have many biblical examples of what it means to be and not to be meek.

In Numbers 12:3 Moses was described as being a "very meek" man, and God spoke with Moses "mouth to mouth" (Num. 12:8). Jesus was also "meek and lowly in heart" (Matt. 11:29), and He "made himself of no reputation, and took upon him the form of a servant, and was made in the likeness of men" (Phil. 2:7). This is a contrast to the enemy who said he "will ascend above the heights of the clouds ... [and] be like the most High" (Isa. 14:14).

Unfortunately, self-exaltation can ignite strife as the person who seeks to be exalted may start a conflict. This is seen in Revelation 12:7–9 when the enemy rose up against God's kingdom and was cast out of heaven. But unlike the enemy, we should constantly strive to consider other people's desires and feelings when making decisions. Second Timothy 2:25 explains that the spirit of meekness is also to be reflected in how we deal with persons who hold a different view to ours. While speaking of our Christian beliefs, we are to display meekness (see 1 Peter 3:15).

The opposite of meekness, as we have seen in the enemy's actions, is pride. Prides makes us believe that we can take the credit for our abilities and our success. First Corinthians 10:12, which states, "Wherefore let him that thinketh he standeth take heed lest he fall," cautions us against being over confident, and Proverbs 3:7 advises us to "be not wise in [our] own eyes." Since Proverbs 16:18 tells us, "Pride goeth before destruction, and an haughty spirit before a fall," we can see that meekness will help us to avoid many pitfalls and heartaches in life.

The attitude of meekness reminds us that we are dust (see Gen. 2:7; Ps. 103:14) and helps us to avoid the sins that occur because of overconfidence. Proverbs 29:23 says, "A man's pride shall bring him low: but honour shall uphold the humble in spirit," and Proverbs 18:12 states that "before honour is humility." Meekness gives us the understanding that the credit for our abilities and success belongs to God. It reminds us that we succeed and overcome only because of God.

Lack of confidence in one's wisdom, however, should not be shifted to full-fledged confidence in everything others say. We are not to trust blindly and completely in human logic and wisdom. We all need to assess the opinions of others based on the Word of God. But pride can prevent us from listening to sound wisdom since we are clouded by the idea that we know and understand every thing. Moses listened to his father-in-law's wise advice (see Exod. 18:13–24), which resulted in the inclusion of other persons to help Moses in addressing the needs of the people. This reduced the burden that Moses carried (see Exod. 18:25, 26).

The Holy Spirit will help us find the balance we need. As we listen to the Holy Spirit's promptings, we acknowledge the limitations of human nature, the true condition of the human heart, and the infiniteness of God's power. We meekly acknowledge our need for divine intervention and for God's continual involve-

> *Meekness allows us to see our worth only when looking through the lens of the sacrifice Jesus made to save us.*

ment in our lives and in all our activities. Meekness allows us to see our worth only when looking through the lens of the sacrifice Jesus made to save us. And realizing the sad state of our hearts without God's intervention (see Rom. 7:24), we cling to the gift of life provided in Christ. We see everything relative to God, and this produces a spirit of humility. In our meekness we can accept that life revolves around God alone.

Temperance

*"And every man that striveth for the mastery is
temperate in all things."* 1 Corinthians 9:25

Temperance is demonstrated in the use of our time and resources as well as the level of discipline we display. When someone is seeking to achieve specific goals, that person will not live a life of excess but will seek to balance his or her life, investing the necessary time and energy to train and develop his or her skills and talents.

Imagine seeing a person conscious of maintaining a proper diet, getting adequate sleep, and reducing the amount of time on things or activities that will distract from his or her success. When an individual knows that his or her body is the temple of the Holy Spirit (see 1 Cor. 6:19), this knowledge also helps the individual to appreciate how to treat his or her body. So an attitude of temperance will be displayed in how we treat our bodies, and we will actively decide not to abuse our bodies.

In a busy world balance can seem illusive, but being temperate each day means consistently getting enough rest and exercise, maintaining a balanced diet, and finding a balance between work and our home life. Temperance is to be a part of our lifestyle and not simply practiced to achieve goals from time to time. This balance is also important to achieve the abundant life.

Without temperance, persons become excessive and get wrapped up in issues like gluttony and greed. Intemperance can also show itself in a person's life by becoming indifferent to the needs of others. A constant preoccupation to acquire the things of this world can lead to an imbalance in thinking, which can result in an imbalance in action.

We need to make the best use of our time. This matters to God. Athletes go into strict discipline. They must have the proper diet, exercise, sleep, training, and mental preparation in order to win the game. We, as Christians, are looking to win the prize of Christ to fulfill our calling (1 Cor. 9:24; Phil. 3:14). Our first priority is to obey God, so we must discipline ourselves and listen steadily for His voice. If we desire to live a life filled with temperance, we should live according to the principles God has outlined for us.

Section 6:

Restored and Whole in Christ

God Revives and Keeps Us

"Now unto him that is able to keep you from falling, and to present you faultless before the presence of his glory with exceeding joy, to the only wise God our Saviour, be glory and majesty, dominion and power, both now and for ever."
Jude 1:24, 25

While transplanting some seedlings, I realized that two of the seedlings were very limp, and I did not have much hope in them ever reviving, but I decided to try nevertheless. I carefully removed them from the seedling tray and placed them in the soil that I had prepared and watered them. The following day I was surprised to see the same plants looking revived and alive. No one would ever have imagined that the plants were so close to death just about fourteen hours before.

Then God reminded me that He has done exactly that for every single one of us countless times; He has revived us. When we feel like we are at the end of the rope and there is no hope, if we accept God's salvation, the Holy Spirit will water our souls, and we will be revived; we will thrive and bear fruit. Jeremiah tells us, "It is of the LORD's mercies that we are not consumed, because his compassions fail not. They are new every morning: great is thy faithfulness" (Lam. 3:22, 23). Every day we are alive, we are alive because of God's grace and breath in us.

> *The nine interconnected attributes of the fruit of the Spirit combine to produce a lifestyle, and this is the newness and daily renewal of life.*

It is not unusual to see persons display great faith, endurance, discipline, and self-control to achieve desired objectives or a future success. But our focus has been on the display of these attributes as a result of the love of God working in and changing our hearts. Being connected to Christ through the Holy Spirit's leading, alone, can produce the complete manifestation of the attributes and components of the fruit in us. Ripe fruit results from the growth of the plant; ripe fruit shows life. A branch connected to the vine (Jesus) continually produces fruit.

The nine interconnected attributes of the fruit of the Spirit combine to produce a lifestyle, and this is the newness and daily renewal of life. It is the culture of God's followers and the universal language that Christians speak. It is Christian knowledge in action. Like a doctor or lawyer, a Christian must practice his or her profession. Christian fruit shows whose we are.

Romans 5:1 states, "Therefore being justified by faith, we have peace with God through our Lord Jesus Christ." When we have experienced God's grace and have accepted His gift of salvation by faith, we "will joy in the God of [our] salvation" (Hab. 3:18). We will hold onto God's peace despite the challenges faced because we understand that nothing "shall be able to separate us from the love of God, which is in Christ Jesus our Lord" (Rom. 8:39).

Once this is fully realized, we will be able to display longsuffering as we wait on God. Isaiah 40:31 says, "They that wait upon the LORD shall renew their strength; they shall mount up with wings as eagles." We will also display patience to others (see 1 Thess. 5:14). We, like Jesus, will display gentleness, and our lives will be filled with good works. Matthew 5:16 states, "Let your light so shine before men, that they may see your good works, and glorify your Father which is in heaven." As we understand that all this can only be achieved because of God, in a spirit of meekness, we will be like Moses and be humble before God (see Num. 12:3). We will seek to utilize God's resources and treat our bodies and others in the way that will glorify our Creator, and we will be temperate in all our undertakings (see 1 Cor. 9:25).

As God's children we look upward in faith to connect and commune with God. We also look inwards as the Holy Spirit's leading results in continued growth in our lives, and we look outward to share God's love with others.

God's Fulfillment of His Promises

*"And God shall wipe away all tears from their
eyes; and there shall be no more death, neither sorrow, nor crying, neither shall there be
any more pain: for the former things are passed
away." Revelation 21:4*

The writings of the prophets in the Old Testament give us a glimpse of the yearning and anticipation God's people had as they looked forward to Jesus' fulfillment of His promise to save us. In Isaiah 9:6 we read, "For unto us a child is born, unto us a son is given: and the government shall be upon his shoulder: and his name shall be called Wonderful, Counsellor, The mighty God, The everlasting Father, The Prince of Peace." Job also stated, "For I know that my redeemer liveth, and that he shall stand at the latter day upon the earth" (Job 19:25). God provided the reassurance that sin was not the end and that the descendent of Eve would overcome the enemy (see Gen. 3:15).

In Luke 2:25, 26 we are told that Simeon had been waiting to see Jesus. When Joseph and Mary took Him to the temple and Simeon saw Jesus, Simeon took Jesus "up in his arms, and blessed God, and said, Lord, now lettest ... thy servant depart in peace, according to thy word: For mine eyes have seen thy salvation" (Luke 2:27–30). Anna, a prophetess, also acknowledged Jesus' presence and "gave thanks likewise unto the Lord, and spake of him to all them that looked for redemption in Jerusalem" (Luke 2:38). When John saw Jesus, John said, "Behold the Lamb of God, which taketh away the sin of the world" (John 1:29). There are many biblical examples to show that God fulfilled and continues to fulfill His promises.

God constantly reminds us that He found a way not to discard us when sin entered into the world. He loves us so much, and we are a part of His family. Jesus was willing to endure the pain to save us. We know that even when we experience scars, challenges, and brokenness in our lives, if we accept God's plan of salvation, God will mend us. Thankfully, the Holy Spirit will always continue the growth process in us each day as we walk along the Christian path.

One week leading up to Independence Day, I heard the sound of drums while I was at work. When I looked outside the office, I saw children marching two by two. The older children were holding the hands of the younger ones, and they were proudly wearing their national colors and carrying flags in their hands. It was then that God reminded me of another city of which I am a citizen "whose builder and maker is God" (Heb. 11:10), and I felt peace thinking about the heavenly home. I wondered what colors and appearance the flag of heaven will carry. What will be the anthem, the motto, and the pledge? I contemplated Jesus' words in John 14:3 where He says He is going to "prepare a place for" us. This text helps us realize that we belong to Him, and we are accepted by Him, and this gives us peace. It is reassuring that Jesus continually exchanges the ashes in our lives and gives us beauty instead (Isa. 61:3). We are free in His love for us.

We can look forward to learning the national anthem of heaven. During the Olympics we see athletes representing their countries when they win medals for their countries. We see the look of pride when their flags are raised and their national anthems are played. When we overcome each of us will become one of God's many trophies to show the universe that God's "grace is sufficient" to free us from sin (2 Cor. 12:9).

Having God in our lives means we can enjoy the freedom from being controlled by passions, self-centeredness, and the desire for self-justification. We are free from the weight of sin through the blood of the Lamb! God made me realize that the independence ceremonies we celebrate on this earth are a sign of the yearning we all have to be

We are at peace when the Holy Spirit is our Master.

truly free. But when we fight against the liberation God has for us and refuse the independence He wants us to experience, we become slaves to our compulsions, addictions, tempers, and to our self-justification. We become a slave to self and only go deeper and deeper into this state. We would become a slave to defending and fighting for ourselves with no real knowledge of the depth and breadth and height of our enemy. God gives us such a higher purpose, and His freedom gives us the peace we crave.

We are at peace when the Holy Spirit is our Master. We can be sure "that he [who] hath begun a good work in [us] will perform it until the day of Jesus Christ" (Phil. 1:6). In Revelation 3:5 Jesus tells us, "He that overcometh, the same shall be clothed in white raiment; and I will not blot out his name out of the book of life, but I will confess his name before my Father, and before His angels." In Revelation 21:2 we read, "John saw the holy city, new Jerusalem, coming down from God out of heaven, prepared as a bride adorned for her husband." We can be comforted by the assurance that God will dwell with His people, and "God shall wipe away all tears from their eyes" (Rev. 21:4).

One day we will be able to say, like Paul, "I have fought a good fight, I have finished my course, I have kept the faith: Henceforth there is laid up for me a crown of righteousness, which the Lord, the righteous judge, shall give me at that day: and not to me only, but unto all them also that love his appearing" (2 Tim. 4:7, 8). As athletes of the cross, as we stand at attention showing our allegiance to God, we will be happy to hear the anthem of heaven and be given "a crown of life" (Rev. 2:10).

We can't fully comprehend what it will be like to finally see Jesus, our Redeemer, face to face, the Person we have heard so much about, and to look into His eyes of perfect love. It will be a wonderful time. Revelation 22:7, 12 says, "Behold, I come quickly." Jesus' return is worth living for. Let us resolve, whatever our situation, that we will be there to sing the anthem of heaven.

We invite you to view the complete
selection of titles we publish at:

www.TEACHServices.com

Scan with your mobile
device to go directly
to our website.

Please write or e-mail us your praises, reactions, or
thoughts about this or any other book we publish at:

TEACH Services, Inc.
P U B L I S H I N G
www.TEACHServices.com • (800) 367-1844

P.O. Box 954
Ringgold, GA 30736

info@TEACHServices.com

TEACH Services, Inc., titles may be purchased in bulk for
educational, business, fund-raising, or sales promotional use.
For information, please e-mail:

BulkSales@TEACHServices.com

Finally, if you are interested in seeing
your own book in print, please contact us at

publishing@TEACHServices.com

We would be happy to review your manuscript for free.